THE NEW TESTAMENT

D1010083

SPARK PUBLISHING

© 2002, 2007 by Spark Publishing

SPARKNOTES is a registered trademark of SparkNotes LLC

Spark Publishing
A Division of Barnes & Noble
120 Fifth Avenue
New York, NY 10011
www.sparknotes.com

ISBN-13: 978-1-4114-0388-8
ISBN-10: 1-4114-0388-6

Please submit changes or report errors to www.sparknotes.com/errors.

Printed in the United States.

10 9 8 7 6

CONTENTS

CONTEXT

THE NEW TESTAMENT IS THE SECOND, shorter part of the Christian Bible. Unlike the Old Testament, which covers hundreds of years of history, the New Testament only covers several decades, and is a collection of the religious teachings and beliefs of Christianity. The New Testament is not a single book written by one person, but, rather, a collection of twenty-seven books written in Greek by people from various places. There are many ways to interpret the New Testament. Millions of people view it as absolutely true scripture, and use its teachings as the basis of their belief systems. Some biblical scholars interpret it as a work of literature that uses beautiful poetry to describe religious myths. Others study its ethical and philosophical ideas, as its stories of the faithful attempt to instill certain values and outline an appropriate way to live.

The books of the New Testament were written in first- or second-century Palestine, a region that at the time was under the rule of the Roman Empire. Many of the stories are based on the rituals and beliefs of Judaism, as Jesus Christ and his disciples were all Jews. As a result, both Greco-Roman culture and Judaic traditions dominate the political, social, and economic scene of the New Testament. Judaism at that time was not a single tradition or set of beliefs, but contained many different divisions within itself. These divisions figure prominently in New Testament stories. The strictest Jews, the Sadducees, were the upper class of priests. They interpreted scripture literally and adhered to rituals strictly. They were opposed to oral tradition and to the concept of eternal life, since the latter is not discussed in the Hebrew Bible, or Old Testament. The Pharisees, in contrast to the Sadducees, interpreted Jewish law for laypeople and established Jewish life outside of the temple. They were more liberal in their acceptance of scripture, regarding oral tradition and the words of prophets as scriptural as well.

Judaism at the time of Christ involved a rigid social hierarchy. The temple and the high priests who worked there were considered to be pure, holy, and closer to God than anyone else. The hierarchy continued with people who were Jews by birth, followed by converts to Judaism. Gentiles, or non-Jews, were considered by Jews to be ritually impure and not in the service of God. The New Testament documents a shift in this hierarchy. Christians challenged the system in which birth into the Israelite community determined a person's level of purity. They said, instead, that repentance and acceptance of the teachings of Jesus Christ determined a person's purity.

The writers of the books that now comprise the New Testament did not intend for their writings to replace or rival the Old Testament. The Christian scriptures were originally intended to be utilitarian documents, responding to specific needs of the early church. It was only with the passage of more than a hundred years after Jesus's death that Christians began to use the term "New Testament" to refer to the scriptures that the fledgling church was beginning to view as a single sacred unit. Early Christians viewed the New Testament as the fulfillment of promises made in the Old Testament, rather than as the replacement of the Jewish scriptures.

The historical context of the New Testament greatly influences the way we interpret it as literature. Many of the speakers in the Bible address issues and problems unique to their moment in history, and a knowledge of the various cultural forces of biblical times provides a basis for understanding the characters' motivations and reactions. Furthermore, the New Testament's role as influential religious doctrine is another context. Just as historical situations shaped the development of the New Testament, the New Testament has also influenced the progress of history. Reading religious documents as literature requires an unusual understanding of the events surrounding the writing of the text.

STRUCTURE AND COMPOSITION

Only in the second century A.D. did Christians begin to use the term "New Testament" to refer to their collection of scriptures. The New Testament as we now know it is comprised of twenty-seven books, but it was not originally written as a coherent whole. Jesus himself did not produce any written record of his work. The books that comprise the New Testament were mostly written in the century following his death, in response to specific needs of the early church and its leaders. At the time of Jesus's crucifixion in approximately 30 A.D., most of the first generation of Christians believed that the end of the world was imminent. They therefore considered it unnecessary to compose records of Jesus's life. By the mid-60s A.D., however, most Christians who had known Jesus and witnessed his actions firsthand were dying. It became necessary, then, to produce works that would testify to Jesus's life. As it became clear that the second coming of Jesus would be delayed, the leaders of the church began to compose works that would enable the nascent Christian Church to survive.

The books that comprise the New Testament can be separated into three broad categories. First are the four Gospels: Matthew, Mark, Luke, and John. "Gospel" literally means "good news." The "good news" to which these gospels refer is the life, teachings, crucifixion, and resurrection of Jesus of Nazareth. The Gospels usually appear first among the texts of the New Testament, with Matthew placed first of all. But the order of the New Testament is based on importance, not chronology. The Gospels were probably written between 65 and 110 A.D., with Mark written first and John last.

The second category of texts in the New Testament are the letters from Paul. Paul of Tarsus was an early church leader and energetic missionary who spread the Gospel of Jesus across the Roman Empire, preaching to Gentiles as well as to Jews, who were the earliest targets of missionary activity. Paul wrote many letters to various Christian communities throughout the Mediterranean, settling points of doctrine and instructing new Christians in matters of faith. By the end of the second century A.D., Christian communities had collected thirteen letters that they attributed to Paul, and each letter became known by the name of the community or individual to whom it was addressed: Romans, 1 and 2 Corinthians, Galatians, Ephesians, Philippians, Colossians, 1 and 2 Thessalonians, 1 and 2 Timothy, Titus, and Philemon. A fourteenth letter, Hebrews, long accepted by Eastern churches, was accepted by Western churches in the fourth century A.D. The actual authorship and date of composition of many of these letters is seriously disputed, but it is generally agreed that Paul wrote some of them in the 50s A.D., making them the oldest existing Christian texts.

Other books in the New Testament are somewhat harder to classify. Acts of the Apostles (known simply as Acts) is a continuation of the Gospel According to Luke, giving the history of the church in the years after Jesus's crucifixion. Acts traces the expansion of the church, as it moves out from Jerusalem and spreads throughout the Gentile world. The protagonists of the book are Peter, the chief of the Twelve Apostles, who were Jesus's closest disciples, and Paul of Tarsus, the greatest early Christian missionary. Also included in the New Testament are seven letters, known as the Letters to all Christians, or the Catholic—in its literal sense, meaning "universal"—Letters, which resemble extended homilies. These letters are generally understood to have been written after the Pauline letters: James, 1 and 2 Peter, 1, 2 and 3 John, and Jude. Finally, the Book of Revelation, written in the closing years of the first century, is an extended vision predicting the events of the end of the world and the second coming of Jesus.

In its early centuries, the church was highly decentralized. Each individual church community collected its own sacred documents. The fragmented nature of the church was complicated by the difference in intellectual tradition between the East, which spoke Greek as its scholarly language and was ruled from Byzantium following the division of the Roman Empire, and the West, which spoke Latin and was centered in Rome. The process by which individual church communities came together to decide on a canon of sacred works, and the process by which they preserved those works, is not entirely clear. Criteria that seem to have been important in canonization include the authorship of the texts—texts presumed to have been written by apostles, such as Matthew, or by those who witnessed Jesus's revelation firsthand, such as Paul, were given priority—and the importance and wide acceptance of the doctrine expressed in the texts. It is known that in the decades just before and after 200 A.D., church leaders widely accepted the sacred nature of a collection of twenty works, including the four Gospels, thirteen Pauline letters, Acts, 1 Peter, and 1 John. The remaining seven works—Hebrews, Revelation, James, 2 and 3 John, Jude, and 2 Peter—were cited from the second to the fourth centuries and accepted as scripture in some, but not all, churches. Finally, by the late fourth century, there was wide, but not absolute, agreement in the Greek East and the Latin West on a canon of twenty-seven works.

It is generally agreed that the books of the New Testament were originally written in Greek, the scholarly language current at the time, and divided into chapters and verses. It is possible that a few books of the New Testament were originally written in Aramaic, a dialect popular among the Jews of Palestine, and most likely the language that Jesus himself spoke.

Plot Overview

THE NEW TESTAMENT is a collection of twenty-seven books centered on the figure of Jesus of Nazareth. Each of these books has its own author, context, theme, and persuasive purpose. Combined, they comprise one of history's most abundant, diverse, complex, and fascinating texts. The books of the New Testament are traditionally divided into three categories: the Gospels, the Epistles, and the Book of Revelation.

THE GOSPELS AND ACTS OF THE APOSTLES

The Gospels of Matthew, Mark, and Luke are known as the synoptic—meaning "at one look"—Gospels because each one tells a similar story, differing only in some additions, special emphases, and particular omissions according to the interests of the author and the message the text is trying to convey. Each of the synoptic Gospels tells the story of Jesus of Nazareth, including his ministry, gathering of disciples, trial, crucifixion, and, in the case of Matthew and Luke, his resurrection. John is also a Gospel, though it is not placed with the synoptic Gospels because his story is so different. Rather than recording many of the facts about Jesus's life, the Gospel according to John focuses on the mystery and identity of Jesus as the Son of God.

Acts of the Apostles follows John, although it was intended to be the second volume of a single unit beginning with Luke. The same author wrote Luke and Acts consecutively, and while Luke is a Gospel about Jesus, Acts picks up the story at the resurrection, when the early disciples are commissioned to witness to the world. Acts is a chronological history of the first church of Christ.

THE EPISTLES

The twenty-one books following Acts are epistles, or letters, written from church leaders to churches in various parts of the world. The first fourteen of these letters are called the "Epistles of Paul" and are letters that tradition has accorded to St. Paul in his correspondence with the earliest churches in the first and second century. Historians are fairly certain that Paul himself, Christianity's first theologian and successful missionary, indisputably composed seven of the letters, and possibly could have written seven others.

The seven letters following the Epistles of Paul are called the Catholic Epistles, because they are addressed to the church as a whole rather than to particular church communities. These letters identify as their authors original apostles, biological brothers of Jesus, and John the Evangelist, although it is thought that they were actually written by students or followers of these early church luminaries. The first of the Catholic Epistles is the Letter of James, attributed to James, the brother of Jesus and leader of the Christian church in Jerusalem. Next are the First and Second Letters of Peter, which identify themselves as letters from the apostle Peter. The First, Second, and Third Letters of John attribute their authorship to John the Evangelist, and the Letter of Jude attributes itself to Jude, the brother of James, who is elsewhere identified as one of Jesus's brothers.

THE REVELATION TO JOHN

The last book in the New Testament is the Revelation to John, or Book of Revelation, the New Testament's only piece of literature in the apocalyptic genre. It describes a vision by a leader of a church community in Asia Minor living under the persecution of the Roman Empire.

Character List

Jesus of Nazareth The central figure of the New Testament, whose life, death, and resurrection are chronicled in the books. The four Gospels describe Jesus's life until his resurrection, and the remainder of the New Testament concerns itself with the community of followers of Jesus that steadily grows after his death.

Paul of Tarsus More than half of the books in the New Testament have been attributed to Paul of Tarsus, the great missionary who directs the spread of Christianity after the death of Jesus. In these books, Paul uses his keen mind and robust intellect to develop Christianity's first sophisticated theology. In the period immediately following Jesus's death, he is an active persecutor of Jesus's followers, but he later converts and becomes the most active proponent of Christ's disciples.

Peter The first of Jesus's disciples. Extremely devoted to Jesus and his mission, Simon is able to recognize Jesus as the Messiah before the other apostles. As a result, Jesus makes him the "rock"—renaming Simon "Peter," which means rock—on which his church would be built (Matthew 16:13–20). Although Peter denies his association with Jesus after Jesus's arrest, Peter later becomes one of the leaders of the church in Jerusalem.

John the Baptist The forerunner to Jesus, spreading the word of Jesus's imminent arrival. John the Baptist is an old ascetic who lives in the desert, wears a loincloth, and feeds on locusts and honey.

Mary Magdalene A female follower of Jesus since the time of his Galilean ministry, when he exorcises her of seven demons (Luke 8:2). Mary Magdalene is a close friend of Jesus. She is one of the women who discover that

Jesus's body is not in his grave. Following this event, she witnesses the resurrected Jesus. She is also known as Mary of Magdala.

Pontius Pilate As prefect, Pontius Pilate governs Judea by the authority of the Roman Empire during the time of Jesus's trial in Jerusalem. The Gospels differ on the extent of Pilate's responsibility for Jesus's crucifixion. What is clear, however, is that Pilate holds the ultimate authority to determine whether or not Jesus should be executed.

Barnabas Praised early in Acts for his generosity toward the church, Barnabas later becomes one of Paul's traveling companions and fellow missionaries, joining Paul in spreading the Gospel among the Gentiles.

Judas Iscariot One of the Twelve Apostles, Judas betrays Jesus to the authorities in exchange for thirty pieces of silver. According to Matthew, Judas commits suicide out of remorse (Matthew 27:3–10).

Stephen A leader of the Hellenists, a faction of the Jewish Christians, in Jerusalem during the years after Jesus's ascension. Stephen preaches against the temple (Acts 6–7). When brought for trial before the Jewish court, Stephen seals his fate by issuing a ringing condemnation of the Jewish leadership.

Timothy The traveling companion and fellow missionary of Paul. Timothy coauthors letters with Paul—such as 1 Corinthians and Philippians—and serves as his emissary throughout the Christian communities of the Mediterranean.

Mary, Mother of Jesus Luke's narrative of Jesus's infancy focuses heavily on the courage and faith of Mary, who becomes impregnated by the Holy Spirit. She is also one of the only people who remains with Jesus through the crucifixion. Gospel writers who have a high esteem for the female leaders in the early church community point to Mary as a model of discipleship.

Joseph   Mary's husband. Joseph is a direct paternal descendent of the great King David, which makes Jesus an heir to the Davidic line. This heritage reinforces Jesus's place in the Jewish tradition.

Luke   A traveling companion of Paul. Christian tradition dating back to the second century A.D. claims that Luke is the author of the Gospel that bears his name and of Acts of the Apostles.

Caiaphas   The high priest who presides over Jesus's trial. Though it is Pilate who declares the verdict of Jesus's guilt, the Gospel writers are insistent that Caiaphas is also responsible for the crucifixion.

Herod the Great   The King of Palestine from 37 to 4 B.C. According to Matthew, Herod hears of Jesus's birth and decides to kill the child, who is prophesied to become king of the Jews. To evade Herod's orders, Joseph takes Jesus and Mary to Egypt.

ANALYSIS OF MAJOR CHARACTERS

JESUS

Jesus's identity is complex and changing throughout the Gospels of the New Testament. Jesus is at once a "bright morning star" (Rev. 22:16) and a small child who worries his mother sick because he stays at the temple for three extra days (Luke 2:46). Jesus is called a "glutton and a drunkard" by those who dislike him (Matthew 11:19), and he breaks social boundaries by associating with women and the poor. Jesus tells a man seeking eternal life to "go, sell what you own, and give the money to the poor, and you will have treasure in heaven; then come, follow me" (Mark 10:21). While Jesus blesses the peace-makers, the meek, and the pure in heart, he overturns the tables of the money changers in the temple, yelling that they have made God's house "a den of robbers" (Mark 11:17). He is simultaneously a "Savior" (Luke 2:11) and a servant who lowers himself to the ground, washing the feet of his disciples (John 13:5). Jesus is bread (John 6:35), light (John 9:1), and water (John 7:38-39). He is also King of Kings, Lord of Lords (Rev. 19:16), and tells a disciple, "[J]ust as you did it to one of the least of these . . . you did it to me" (Matthew 25:40).

PETER

Simon Peter is one of the most sympathetic characters in the entire New Testament. Peter is determined to be Jesus's best disciple, but prematurely thinks he understands what it means to follow Jesus. Peter does not believe Jesus's prediction that he will deny having known Jesus, but Peter's eagerness is immature, and he does end up denying his friendship to Jesus during the terrifying series of events surrounding the trial and crucifixion. Peter realizes his mistake and weeps bitterly. He is forgiven, and remains the rock upon which Jesus says he will build his church. Peter is a model of faithful discipleship. To this day, the Catholic Church claims apostolic succession from this very Peter, whose faith was as solid as a rock, but who was also at times overeager, afraid, and all too human.

PAUL

Paul, an extremely well-educated Jew, is living in Palestine when he receives a vision of Jesus and becomes a follower. Paul, however, continues to call himself the "Jew of Jews." Christianity is indebted to Paul's tireless toil for the Gospel in the first century, and to his robust intellectual prowess, which brings Christianity from a small handful of fringe-society disciples to a church with a sophisticated theology treating such complex issues as the relationship between faith and works, and the balance between unity and diversity. It is clear that Paul, whom some have called "history's first egalitarian," develops an enormous range of church leaders, including many women, in his household churches that peppered the hillsides of the Roman Empire and the coast of the Mediterranean Sea.

CHARACTER ANALYSIS

THEMES, MOTIFS & SYMBOLS

THEMES

Themes are the fundamental and often universal ideas explored in a literary work.

THE NEW TESTAMENT'S RELATION TO THE OLD TESTAMENT

Each of the books of the New Testament has a unique relationship to the Old Testament and to Judaism as a whole, ranging from the very Jewish Gospel of Matthew to the Gospel of Luke, which makes little or no reference to the Jewish scriptures. This range is largely due to the location and audience of the different authors of the New Testament. Matthew's Gospel was written for a largely Jewish group to convince them that Jesus was the hoped-for Messiah, and so he interprets Jesus as someone who relives the experience of Israel. For Matthew, everything about Jesus is prophesied in the Old Testament. The Old Testament narratives to which Matthew refers served as ways in which early followers of Jesus could make sense out of his birth, death, and resurrection. In contrast, Luke makes little or no reference to the Hebrew scriptures because they would have been unfamiliar to his largely Gentile audience.

Paul introduces yet another perspective on the Hebrew Scriptures with his theology of "faith versus works," which states that through Christ we are saved "through grace alone," not through doing good works. Paul contrasts Christianity's emphasis on the grace of God and the faith of the believer with the Jewish insistence on the law as the necessary means for salvation. Paul's theology inaugurates a strong anti-Jewish tradition in Christianity, which claims that Christianity is a higher, more spiritual tradition than Judaism. This claim is called Christian supercessionism because it is based on the idea that the New Testament supercedes the Old Testament. Supercessionists believe that the laws laid down in the Old Testament are external, in the sense that they regulate human behaviors rather than spiritual states, and that these laws become unnecessary through Christ. Supercessionism simplifies the rich and subtle theology of the Old Testament, which makes no such distinction between faith and works.

SALVATION FOR SOCIAL OUTCASTS

Some scholars have argued that the New Testament's references to sinners actually referred to those who were marginalized, poor, cast out, orphaned, diseased, or widowed. Jesus not only promises salvation to such sinners, but goes so far as to call their poverty itself "blessed" throughout the Gospels. At many points in Jesus's ministry, he shocks mainstream Jews by associating with, ministering to, and healing people who are cast out, poor, and sick. Some have argued that a prominent theme in the Gospels is Jesus's good news to such people and an invitation to the rich to join them.

SALVATION THROUGH FAITH IN CHRIST

In his final letter to the new churches in Romans, Paul summarizes his lifelong question about the relationship between Jewish law, which requires certain observances and actions, and faith in the grace offered by God through Jesus Christ, which is given freely and without regard for good works. This issue was particularly problematic in Rome because the early church consisted both of Jewish followers of Christ, who observed the law, and Gentile followers, to whom the law was relatively unknown. Paul concludes that the law is a gift from God, and can help people become more faithful, but ultimately we are justified by faith alone, and the grace of God is available to both Jews and Gentiles. In the end, Paul declares that only minimal observance of Jewish law is necessary to be a follower of Jesus—who himself, interestingly enough, was a law-abiding Jew.

MOTIFS

Motifs are recurring structures, contrasts, and literary devices that can help to develop and inform the text's major themes.

GEOGRAPHY

The Gospel of Mark takes us on a vivid journey through the roads of first-century Palestine, from the small Galilean villages to Jerusalem, where Jesus's trial and crucifixion take place. The shifts from location to location in the narrative are often abrupt and hasty, but these movements serve an important purpose in that they teach believers that Christian discipleship means following in the footsteps of Jesus. Believers are to follow his progress in their imaginations, as one follows a character in a story, sympathizing with him in his progression to the cross. Jesus's trail toward the cross offers a warning to potential followers that discipleship may involve persecution and suffering, and will call for unremitting faithfulness on the part of the disciple.

SYMBOLS

Symbols are objects, characters, figures, and colors used to represent abstract ideas or concepts.

THE KINGDOM OF HEAVEN

The longest section of Matthew's Gospel is his "proclamation" (Matthew 4:17–16:20), in which he issues a number of declarations about the kingdom of heaven. Matthew likens God's kingdom to a small mustard seed, which has in it the potential to grow into a "tree so that the birds of the air come and make nests in its branches," something startlingly different in size and appearance from its humble beginnings. Matthew's proclamations about the kingdom of God symbolize the tantalizing fruits yielded by a life lived in obedience to the commandments of Christ. His use of the phrase "kingdom of heaven" also discloses Matthew's Jewish roots, as in Jewish custom one could not utter God's name.

THE GOOD SAMARITAN

In one of the New Testament's most well known parables, Luke tells us that Jesus used this story as the answer to a man's question, "Who is my neighbor?" Jesus describes a man lying on the road, dying. Neither a passing priest nor a Levite helps him, because touching a dead body was considered utterly impure. The Samaritan, however, rescues the man, thereby breaking two social conventions—associating with what could be a corpse, and crossing the border between the rival communities of Jews and Samaritans. The Samaritan can be understood to symbolize both Christ's message that the poor and outcast are blessed, and that Christ's message is for Gentiles as well as Jews.

WATER, BREAD, LIGHT

In John's Gospel, Jesus is symbolized by the life-giving matter of everyday existence: water, bread, light, and words. Water and bread, in particular, are used repeatedly. While speaking with a Samaritan woman at the well, Jesus tells her, "water that I will give will become in them a spring of water gushing up to eternal life." She says in reply, "[S]ir, give me this water so that I may never be thirsty or have to keep coming here to draw water." John uses this symbol of water to illustrate that Jesus's gift is abundant and life-giving.

THE OLIVE TREE

In Romans 11:17–24, the olive tree symbolizes the salvation of the Gentiles and of Israel. The tree, including the root and branches, is Israel. The branches broken off are the Jews who do not believe in Jesus Christ, while the branches grafted on are Gentiles who believe in Christ. Having been made part of the tree only because of faith—rather than birth, obedience to the law, or works—the Gentile believers have no reason for pride, since the God who has grafted them on has the power to cut them off.

THE BODY

In 1 Corinthians 12:12, Paul writes about the variety of spiritual gifts that exist using the image of the human body to convey that each of these different gifts is needed, just as every part of the body is needed. The church is Christ's body. Paul writes, "For just as the body is one and has many members, all the members of the body, though many, are one body, so it is with Christ. For in the one Spirit we were all baptized into one body—Jews or Greeks, slaves or free—and we were all made to drink of one Spirit." Paul uses this symbol as a way to deal with the difficult issue of balancing unity and diversity in his early churches, saying that though we are all uniquely gifted individuals, we are also all parts of the one united body of Christ.

SUMMARY & ANALYSIS

THE GOSPEL ACCORDING TO MATTHEW (MATTHEW)

> *[T]he Son of man came eating and drinking, and they say, "Look, a glutton and a drunkard, a friend of tax collectors and sinners!" Yet wisdom is vindicated by her deeds.*
>
> *(See* QUOTATIONS, *p. 65)*

INTRODUCTION

In the second century A.D., the Gospel of Matthew was placed at the very beginning of the New Testament. It was believed to be the first Gospel written, though we now know that the Gospel of Mark dates earlier. Because it is the Gospel most intensely concerned with issues related to Judaism, it provides an appropriate transition from the Old Testament to the New Testament in the Christian Bible. Matthew became the most important of all Gospel texts for first- and second-century Christians because it contains all the elements important to the early church: the story about Jesus's miraculous conception; an explanation of the importance of liturgy, law, discipleship, and teaching; and an account of Jesus's life and death. The Gospel of Matthew has long been considered the most important of the four Gospels.

Though second-century church tradition holds that the author of the Gospel is Matthew, a former tax collector and one of Jesus's Twelve Apostles, also known as Levi, scholars today maintain that we have no direct evidence of Matthew's authorship. Because the Gospel of Matthew relies heavily on the earlier Gospel of Mark, as well as late first-century oral tradition for its description of events in Christ's life, it is unlikely that the author of the Gospel of Matthew was an eyewitness to the life of Christ. Instead, the author was probably a Jewish member of a learned community in which study and teaching were passionate forms of piety, and the Gospel was probably written between 80 and 90 A.D.

Matthew is arranged in seven parts. An introductory segment gives the story of Jesus's miraculous birth and the origin of his ministry, and a conclusion gives the story of the Last Supper, Jesus's trial and crucifixion, and the resurrection. In the middle are five structurally parallel sections. In each section, a narrative segment—interrupted occasionally by dialogue and brief homilies—tells of Jesus's miracles and actions. Closing each section, Jesus preaches a long sermon that responds to the lessons learned in the narrative section. The Sermon on the Mount, which introduces the basic elements of the Christian message, follows Jesus's first venture into ministry (5:1–7:29). The Mission Sermon, which empowers Jesus's apostles, follows Jesus's recognition that more teachers and preachers are necessary (10:1–42). The mysterious Sermon in Parables responds to Jesus's frustration with the fact that many people do not understand or accept his message (13:1–52). The Sermon on the Church responds to the need to establish a lasting fraternity of Christians (18:1–35). Finally, the Eschatological Sermon, which addresses the end of the world, responds to the developing certainty that Jesus will be crucified (23:1–25:46)

SUMMARY

Matthew traces Jesus's ancestors back to the biblical patriarch Abraham, the founding father of the Israelite people. Matthew describes Jesus's conception, when his mother, Mary, was "found to be with child from the Holy Spirit" (1:18). Matthew focuses very little on Mary herself, and praises Joseph for not abandoning his fiancée.

Jesus is born in Bethlehem, where he and his parents are visited by wise men from the East bearing gifts. The wise men follow a star to Bethlehem. Their king, Herod the Great, hears the rumor that a baby named Jesus is the "king of the Jews" (2:2). Herod orders all young children in Bethlehem to be killed. To escape the king's wrath, Joseph, Mary, and Jesus flee to Egypt. Joseph and his family return to Israel after Herod's death, but then move to Nazareth, a town in the northern district known as Galilee.

Years pass, and Jesus grows up. A man in a loincloth, who lives by eating wild honey and locusts, begins to prophesy throughout Judea, foretelling of Jesus as the one who will come to "baptize you with the Holy Spirit and fire" (3:11). This prophet, John the Baptist, who is likely a member of the ascetic Jewish Essene community, eventually meets Jesus. John baptizes Jesus, and Jesus receives the blessing of God, who says, "This is my Son, the Beloved" (3:17). Jesus is led into the wilderness for forty days without food or water to be tested by Satan. Jesus emerges unscathed and triumphant, and begins to preach his central, most often repeated proclamation: "Repent! For the kingdom of heaven has come near" (4:17). His ministry begins.

Matthew mentions Jesus's earliest followers: Simon Peter, Andrew, James, and John. Once Jesus accumulates this small group of Jewish followers, he begins to preach. His early ministry reaches a peak when he gives a sermon famously known as the Sermon on the Mount, which deeply impresses his increasingly large group of followers (5:1–7:29). The sermon emphasizes humility, obedience, love of one's neighbor, the proper method of prayer, and trust in God. Jesus says that the poor, meek, and hungry are blessed.

As he travels through Galilee, Jesus continues to attract crowds. Matthew relates ten of Jesus's miracles, which are also described in the Gospel of Mark. Jesus cures a leper, a paralytic, a hemorrhaging woman, a centurion's servant, and Peter's mother-in-law. He also calms a storm, exorcizes demons, gives eyesight to the blind, and brings a dead girl back to life. Jesus resolves to "send out laborers" to minister to the Gentiles, to whom he refers as lost sheep (9:38). Jesus appoints twelve disciples, telling them that they will be persecuted but they should not be afraid. Jesus instructs the apostles to preach that the "kingdom of heaven has come near," and to heal the sick, raise the dead, cleanse lepers, and cast out demons, all without payment (10:7).

In Chapter 11, Matthew interrupts his account of Jesus and his disciples' mission to focus on Jesus himself. He gives an account of the opposition Jesus faces. Some people disapprove of his association with sinners, tax collectors, and prostitutes. They call him a glutton and a drunkard. In the face of such rejection, Jesus does not apologize, but, rather, admonishes those who reject him.

Jesus responds to his challengers with a collection of parables. Matthew describes several of the parables—the parables of the sower, the weeds, the mustard seed, and the leaven—that Jesus tells to the crowds that gather to listen to him (13:1–33). Jesus then explains that his disciples are part of his family.

Jesus's ministry of healing, cleansing, and raising the dead continues as he travels throughout Galilee. But he is rejected in his hometown of Nazareth, where his friends and neighbors deride him. He continues to perform miracles, but the people become increasingly resistant and disbelieving. Jesus multiplies loaves and fish, feeding thousands on very little food. He heals the sick and continues to preach the message of spiritual righteousness. Yet Jesus repeatedly finds that his disciples still lack faith in him. When he miraculously walks across the water to them, they assume he must be a ghost. Even after he multiplies the loaves, they fear hunger. Only Simon properly professes his faith, "You are the Messiah, the Son of the living God" (16:16). Jesus renames Simon "Peter," a name whose Greek form is identical to the Greek word "rock." Jesus announces, "You are Peter, and on this rock I will build my church" (16:18). Jesus then lays out the rules for communal relations among Christians, emphasizing forgiveness, humility, and obedience to his teachings.

Jesus continues to preach. He forbids divorce and advocates chastity, while expounding the virtues of asceticism. He warns against the pitfalls of wealth, teaches forgiveness, and welcomes children. In Jerusalem, cheering crowds await him. People "spread their cloaks on the road, and others cut branches from the trees and spread them on the road" (21:8). Upon his arrival in Jerusalem, Jesus expels money changers from the Jewish temple and defies the chief priests and elders, saying, "My house shall be called a house of prayer, but you are making it a den of robbers" (21:13). Jesus's action earns him the support of the crowds. He chastises Jewish leaders, telling them they have been poor caretakers of the temple and that the people have been hypocritical, focusing on technical legal issues rather than "justice and mercy and faith" (23:23). Seeing the wickedness of Jerusalem, and foreseeing God's punishment of the wicked, Jesus warns his disciples to be prepared for the end of the world. He says that tribulations will precede the final judgment, but that the Son of man—Jesus himself—will come, and that the righteous will be saved.

In Chapter 26, Jesus celebrates the Last Supper with the disciples. Jesus indicates that Judas, one of his disciples, will betray him. Jesus predicts that after his death, the other disciples will flee, and Peter will also betray him. When he breaks bread and drinks wine with the disciples, Jesus initiates a ritual that later becomes known as the Eucharist, the consumption of bread and wine symbolizing Jesus's body and blood. After dining with the apostles, Jesus goes into a garden called Gethsemane. There he prays, asking God if it is possible to escape the impending suffering. As Jesus is leaving the garden, Judas approaches, accompanied by a mob and a great number of Roman soldiers. Judas kisses Jesus in order to show the angry mob which man claims to be the Son of God.

Jesus is arrested and brought before the Jewish court, where he is convicted of blasphemy. Caiaphas, the high priest, sends him to

Pontius Pilate, the governor of Rome, for a final verdict. Pilate looks surprisingly weak and undecided. He turns to the crowd for the judgment and they all chant, "Let him be crucified!" (27:22). Pilate concedes. Jesus is led out, crowned with thorns, mocked, and crucified. On the cross, Jesus cries out, "My God, my God, why have you forsaken me?" and then dies (27:46). Matthew notes the presence of "many women" at the execution, including "Mary Magdalene, and Mary the mother of James and Joseph, and the mother of the sons of Zebedee" (27:56). Jesus is buried by Joseph of Arimathea and a guard is set over the tomb. On the first day of the week, three days after the crucifixion, Mary Magdalene and Mary go to visit Jesus's tomb in order to anoint his body with oils and spices according to Jewish custom, but they find the tomb empty. Astonished, they see an angel who tells them that Jesus has been resurrected from the dead and that he can be found in Galilee. The women leave the tomb both happy and afraid. Suddenly, Jesus greets them and asks them to tell his disciples to meet him in Galilee. After the women leave, the guards tell the city's chief priests what has happened, and the priests bribe the guards to report that Jesus's body was stolen while they were sleeping. In Galilee, Jesus commissions his disciples to teach and baptize nonbelievers as they travel throughout the world.

ANALYSIS

The Gospel of Matthew is strongly connected to the Old Testament. Although Matthew, Mark, Luke, and John all cite Old Testament prophesies that they regard as having been fulfilled in the person and works of Jesus, Matthew is particularly careful to point out that Jesus's teachings are compatible with Judaism, and to insist that Jesus's life fulfills Old Testament prophesies. Matthew portrays Jesus as a second, greater Moses, an important prophet in the Old Testament. Just as Moses gave his law from Mount Sinai in the Old Testament, Jesus preaches his new laws in a sermon he gives from a mountain. Like Moses, the young Jesus hides in Egypt from the wrath of a vengeful king. Finally, Jesus is tempted for forty days and forty nights in the wilderness, while Moses and his people wandered the wilderness for forty years.

Matthew further emphasizes Jesus's ties to Jewish tradition by tracing Jesus's ancestry to Abraham, the father of the Jewish people. Matthew clearly speaks from within the Jewish tradition to a largely Jewish audience. But at the same time, Matthew's Gospel contains some of the most vehement anti-Jewish polemic in the entire New

Testament. For example, Matthew challenges mere external obedience to religious law, valuing instead an internal spiritual transformation: "You have heard that it was said 'You shall love your neighbor and hate your enemy.' But I say to you, Love your enemies and pray for those who persecute you" (5:43). It is also possible to interpret such passages as Jesus's reinterpretation of Jewish law rather than his rejection of it. Jesus is simply reminding his community what Jewish law already indicates: that God demands absolute obedience and not just the appearance of obedience.

Matthew is the most carefully structured of the Gospels: it proceeds through an introduction; five central segments, each designed with a concluding sermon that responds to the concerns raised in the preceding narrative; and a conclusion detailing Jesus's Passion. Matthew's careful construction reflects his Gospel's concern with rhetorical structure. In contrast with Mark's spare style and Luke's formal tone, Matthew's rhetoric is meant to be stirring. Many readers regard the five sermons in which Matthew conveys Jesus's teachings as some of the finest prose in the New Testament. The Sermon on the Mount is Matthew's greatest composition, in which he reveals his talent for epigrams, balanced sentences, and rhetorical shifts as he moves the sermon from its graceful and quietly powerful opening, "Blessed are the poor in spirit, for theirs is the kingdom of heaven" (5:3), to its tempestuous finale, "The rain fell, and the floods came, and the winds blew and beat against that house, and it fell—and great was its fall!" (7:27).

THE GOSPEL ACCORDING TO MARK (MARK)

INTRODUCTION

For a long time, the Gospel of Mark was the least popular of the Gospels, both among scholars and general readers. Mark's literary style is somewhat dull—for example, he begins a great number of sentences with the word "then." Luke and Matthew both contain the same story of Jesus's life, but in more sophisticated prose. Mark also leaves out accounts of Jesus's birth, the Sermon on the Mount, and several of the most well known parables. Mark became more popular, however, when biblical scholars discovered it was the earliest written of the four Gospels, and was probably the primary source of information for the writers of Luke and Matthew. Moreover, because neither Jesus nor his original disciples left any writings behind, the Gospel of Mark is the closest document to an original source on Jesus's life that currently exists. The presumed author of the Gospel of Mark, John Mark, was familiar with Peter, Jesus's closest disciple. Indeed, Mark is the New Testament historian who comes closest to witnessing the actual life of Jesus. Though Mark's Gospel certainly comes to us through his own personal lens, scholars are fairly confident that Mark is a reliable source of information for understanding Jesus's life, ministry, and crucifixion. As a result of its proximity to original sources, the Gospel of Mark has transformed from a book disregarded for its lowly prose to one of the most important books in the New Testament. Its historical importance has affected its evaluation by literary scholars as well. Though crude and terse, the Gospel of Mark is vivid and concrete. Action dominates. A dramatic sense of urgency is present, and Mark has a developed sense of irony that permeates the Gospel.

SUMMARY

The Gospel According to Mark has no story of Jesus's birth. Instead, Mark's story begins by describing Jesus's adult life, introducing it with the words, "The beginning of the good news of Jesus Christ, the Son of God" (1:1). Mark tells of John the Baptist, who predicts the coming of a man more powerful than himself. After John baptizes Jesus with water, the Holy Spirit of God recognizes Jesus as his son, saying, "You are my Son, the Beloved" (1:11). Jesus goes to the wilderness, where Satan tests him for forty days, and Jesus emerges triumphant.

Jesus travels to Galilee, the northern region of Israel. He gathers his first disciples, Simon and Andrew, two Jewish brothers who are both fishermen. Jesus asks them to follow him, saying that he will show them how to fish for people rather than for fish. Simon and Andrew, as well as James and John, drop their nets and follow him. Jesus exhibits his authority in Galilee, where he cleanses a leper (1:40–45). Mark reports that Jesus heals a paralytic, Simon's sick mother-in-law, and a man with a withered hand. The miracles cause the crowds that gather to watch Jesus to become bewildered, fearful, and antagonistic. The Pharisees and followers of Herod begin plotting to kill Jesus. Jesus stays focused on his ministry.

Jesus's ministry attracts many followers. The miracle stories become increasingly longer and more elaborate, emphasizing the supernatural power of Jesus's authority. Mark says that "even wind and sea obey him" (4:35–41). Simultaneously, Jesus becomes increasingly misunderstood and rejected, even by his own apostles.

Jesus notes his disciples' frequent misunderstandings of his message. Jesus's power continues to reveal itself in his control over nature: he calms a storm, cures a man possessed by a demon, and revives a dead young girl. Despite his successes, however, he continues to be reviled in his own hometown of Nazareth.

The story of Jesus's ministry reaches King Herod Antipas, the ruler of Galilee who beheaded John the Baptist. Jesus disperses the apostles, charging them with the responsibility to spread the Gospel and to heal the sick. When the apostles rejoin Jesus, they are once again swarmed with people eager to hear Jesus's message. Through a miracle, Jesus divides five loaves of bread and two fish and feeds all 5,000 people. His disciples, however, seem not to understand the magnitude of his miracle: when he walks on water, they are shocked. The Pharisees, who are upset at Jesus's abandonment of the traditional Jewish laws, question Jesus. He responds by pointing out that it is important to obey the spirit of the law rather than simply going through the technical actions that the law proscribes. Jesus preaches that human intention, not behavior, determines righteousness.

Jesus travels again through northern Palestine. He heals a deaf man and the child of a Gentile, and works a second miracle in which he multiplies a small amount of bread and fish to feed 4,000 people. His disciples, however, continue to misunderstand the significance of his actions. Peter, the foremost of the disciples, seems to be the only one who recognizes Jesus's divine nature. Jesus begins to foresee his own crucifixion and resurrection. He continues to travel across Galilee, but shifts his emphasis to preaching rather than working miracles. He appears to some of his disciples to be transfigured, made brilliantly white. Jesus explains that John the Baptist served as his Elijah, predicting his arrival. He preaches against divorce and remarriage. He announces that young children, in their innocence, are models for righteous behavior, and that the rich will have great difficulty entering the kingdom of God. He teaches, despite the sacrifices necessary to enter the kingdom, it will be worth it: "Many who are first will be last, and the last, first" (10:31).

Finally, Jesus journeys to Jerusalem, where he drives the money changers from the temple and begins preaching his Gospel. He is well received by the common people but hated by the priests and the scribes. However, he successfully defends himself against the priests' verbal attacks. He teaches that obedience to Caesar is important, that the dead will be resurrected, that loving one's neighbor is the greatest commandment, and that the End of Days will soon come, bringing God's retribution on the unjust and the return of the Son of man.

Eventually, Jesus allows himself to succumb to the conspiracy against him. At the Passover Seder, Jesus institutes the Christian sacrament of the Eucharist, telling his followers to eat and drink his symbolic body and blood. At the dinner, Jesus says that one of his disciples will betray him. The disciples are surprised, each asking, "Surely, not I?" (14:19). After dinner, Jesus goes to a garden called Gethsemane and prays while Peter, James, and John wait nearby. The three disciples fall asleep three times, though Jesus returns each time and asks them to stay awake with him as he prays. Jesus prays to God that, if possible, he might avoid his imminent suffering.

Jesus is leaving the garden with Peter, James, and John when Judas Iscariot, one of the apostles, arrives with the city's chief priests and a crowd carrying swords and clubs. Judas kisses Jesus, indicating to the priests Jesus's identity. The priests arrest Jesus and take him to the court of the high priest. There, Jesus publicly claims that he is "the Messiah, the Son of the Blessed One," and the Jews deliver him to Pontius Pilate, the Roman governor, who agrees to crucify him (14:61). On the cross, Jesus cries out, "My God, my God, why have you forsaken me?" (15:34). He dies and is buried by Joseph of Arimathea, a righteous Jew. When Mary Magdalene and other women come to Jesus's grave on the third day after the crucifixion, however, they find it empty. A young man tells them that Jesus has risen from the grave. Jesus then appears in resurrected form to Mary, Mary Magdalene, and the apostles.

SUMMARY & ANALYSIS

ANALYSIS

Mark's Gospel is often disconnected, and at times difficult to read as a logically progressing narrative. This Gospel is brief and concise, reading almost like an outline, with little effort made to connect the roughly chronological list of incidents. Mark's Gospel also tends to interrupt itself by introducing information of marginal relevance. For example, Mark interrupts the story of the dispersal of the apostles and their return with the anecdote about Herod Antipas and John the Baptist. The Gospels of Matthew and Luke rely on Mark for much of their information, and they flesh out the bare-bones outline, adding additional information and employing a more fluid and elaborate style. The relationship between these first three Gospels is extremely complex. They are often approached as a group because of their strong similarities, and because of the way in which they appear to have been influenced by each other or by common sources. Because of their interconnectedness, they are called "synoptic," meaning that they can be looked at "with one glance."

The Gospel of Mark does show some evidence of tight, purposeful construction. Mark can be divided into two sections. The first, from 1:1 to 8:26, concerns itself with Jesus's ministry in Galilee, beginning with John the Baptist's prophecy proclaiming the advent of the Messiah. The second, from 8:27 to 16:20, tells the story of Jesus's prediction of his own suffering, crucifixion, and resurrection.

Mark's Gospel constantly presumes that the end of the world is imminent. Therefore, when the end of time never came, early Christian communities had difficulty interpreting passages such as the thirteenth chapter of Mark, whose apocalyptic vision is urgent, striking, and confident. Another prominent motif of Mark is secrecy. Mark writes that the kingdom is near, the time has come, but only a few are privy to any knowledge of it. This motif is known as the Messianic Secret. For example, Mark refers to secrecy in relation to the kingdom of God in 4:11-12:

> And he said to them, "To you has been given the secret of the kingdom of God, but for those outside everything comes in parables, in order that I 'they may indeed look but not perceive.'"

For Mark, Jesus's parables are riddles meant to be understood only by a select few. However, as the Gospel unfolds, the disciples do not maintain their privileged position.

As Mark tells his story, the twelve disciples persistently, even increasingly, fail to understand Jesus. Ultimately, two of them betray him, the rest abandon him, and at the end he is crucified alone until two of his bravest disciples, Mary Magdalene and Mary, return and find his tomb empty. If anyone is loyal in this Gospel, it is the Galilean women who look on Jesus's crucifixion from a distance and come to bury him. The Gospel of Mark is brutal on the disciples; some scholars suggest that Mark is trying to express his theme that when one follows Christ, one must be prepared for the experiences of misunderstanding and even persecution. Mark's model of discipleship includes the experiences of failure and doubt as part of the process of coming to understand the full meaning of Jesus. For Mark, discipleship means debating, questioning, stumbling, and learning. It involves suffering, service to others, poverty, and faithfulness despite persecution. It is strange that the Gospel of Mark ends so abruptly; scholars generally agree that the Gospel of Mark ends with verse 16:8, and that verses 16:9–20 were a later addition to the manuscript. The ending at 16:8 is confusing: Jesus's body is gone, and in his place an angel appears to Mary Magdalene and others, charging them to tell Peter of Jesus's resurrection. The women fail to fulfill this command: "So they went out and fled from the tomb, for the terror and amazement had seized them; and they said nothing to anyone, for they were afraid" (16:8). This ending is hardly triumphant, and verses 16:9–20 preserve Mark's original message. Jesus appears to his apostles, and victory seems assured: "And they went out and proclaimed the good news everywhere, while the Lord worked with them and confirmed the message by the signs that accompanied it" (16:20).

THE GOSPEL ACCORDING TO LUKE (LUKE)

INTRODUCTION

> *A sower went out to sow his seed; and as he sowed,*
> *some fell on the path, and was trampled on, and the*
> *birds of the air ate it up.*
>
> *(See* QUOTATIONS, *p. 68)*

The final editors of the New Testament separated the Gospel According to Luke and Acts of the Apostles, which were originally written by the same author in a single two-volume work. The Gospel of Luke is the unit's first half and narrates the birth, ministry, death, and resurrection of Jesus. The second half, which contains Acts of the Apostles, is one of the first works to chronicle church history, tracing events from the resurrection of Jesus to the time when the apostle Paul is traveling and proclaiming the Gospel "with all boldness and without hindrance" (Acts 28:31). Luke's Gospel features an introductory prologue typical of a historian in antiquity. He writes, "I too, decided, after investigating everything carefully from the very first, to write an orderly account for you, most excellent Theophilus, so that you may know the truth concerning the things about which you have been instructed" (1:3–4). Luke's orderly account relies on eyewitnesses of Jesus and the earliest disciples, though he could not have been an eyewitness himself. The Gospel of Luke dates from between 75 and 85 A.D., around the same time as Matthew. The author relies most likely on the Gospel of Mark and other stories circulating orally during his lifetime. Luke's Greek is the polished work of a gifted literary artist, indicating that Luke was a cultivated, well-educated man.

SUMMARY

After his introduction, Luke lays out, in two chapters, the parallel miraculous births of Jesus of Nazareth and the man who becomes his prophet, John the Baptist. The angel Gabriel appears to Zechariah, telling him that his wife Elizabeth, formerly barren, is pregnant. Soon afterward, Gabriel appears to Elizabeth's relative, the virgin Mary, who is betrothed to Joseph, telling her that she too is going to give birth to a child by the grace of the Holy Spirit. Mary visits Elizabeth, and Elizabeth prophesies that Mary will be "the mother of my Lord" (1:43). Mary, rejoicing, utters the prayer now known as the Magnificat: "My soul magnifies the Lord" (1:46). John is born, and his father, Zechariah—who had been struck mute for the duration of the pregnancy as a punishment for his lack of belief in Gabriel's prophecy—utters a prayer, the Benedictus: "Blessed be the Lord, God of Israel . . ." (1:68). Mary and Joseph travel from their home in Nazareth to Bethlehem to partake in a census, and there, in a manger, Jesus is born. When Jesus is presented at the temple, where all firstborn males are brought, two Jewish prophets, Simeon and Anna, recognize the sanctity of the child. As yet, however, nobody realizes his true significance. When Mary finds the adolescent Jesus sitting in the temple among the sages, she does not understand his remark, "Why were you searching for me? Did you not know I must be in my Father's house?" (2:49).

Jesus grows to maturity and is baptized in the desert of Judea by John the Baptist, who has begun his advocacy of baptismal repentance for the forgiveness of sins, and prophesies the advent of Jesus. John, however, is soon imprisoned by Herod Antipas, the ruler of the northern Galilee region. After Jesus's baptism, Luke gives Jesus's genealogy, stretching back to the first man, Adam, who is said to be "son of God" (3:38). We are told of Satan unsuccessfully testing Jesus for forty days in the wilderness. Returning from the wilderness, Jesus begins his ministry. He is rejected in his hometown of Nazareth and takes to wandering throughout Galilee, where he works many miracles, including the exorcism of a demoniac and many other cures. He works a miracle enabling Simon Peter, a fisherman, to catch many fish, and thereby attracts Simon Peter, as well as James and John, the sons of Zebedee, as his first apostles. Later, these three apostles are joined by nine others. In this first stage of his ministry, Jesus also begins to encounter opposition from the Pharisees, who question his adherence to traditional Jewish laws governing Sabbath observance, fasting, and consorting with sinners.

Despite this opposition, his fame grows, and he attracts a great crowd to whom he delivers a shorter version of Matthew's great Sermon on the Mount, telling his followers to "love your enemies, do good to those who hate you" (6:27).

Jesus goes to Capernaum, where he cures the servant of a Roman centurion and restores the son of a widow to life. When John the Baptist, imprisoned, sends messengers to ask Jesus who he is, Jesus responds only by pointing out the many miracles he has worked. Jesus commends John the Baptist's ministry and laments the fact that his contemporaries have refused to listen to John and to Jesus himself. Jesus's travels continue as he preaches and works miracles. Accepting the ministrations of a wicked woman, Jesus shows that he forgives even the most wretched of sinners. He explains in a parable that the seed of the word of God will only sprout in noble and generous hearts, and that the true family of Jesus is not his mother and siblings, but those who hear the word of God. Among his miracles, he calms a storm; cures a man possessed by a demon, and a woman with a hemorrhage; and revives the daughter of Jairus. Jesus sends the Twelve Apostles out to preach the Gospel and to cure illness. On their return, Jesus is swarmed by people eager to hear his preaching. He works the miracle of the loaves and fish for them, multiplying scant food to feed 5,000 people. When he questions the faith of his apostles, asking, "Who do you say that I am?", Peter replies, "The Messiah of God" (9:20). Immediately after this event, Jesus gives the first of his three prophecies of the Passion, during which he predicts that he will be executed and resurrected. A set of brief spiritual messages ensues: following Christ means a total abnegation of the self; the kingdom of God is imminent; and humility is crucial, as "the least among all of you is the greatest" (9:48).

Jesus begins to travel toward Jerusalem. His journey is punctuated by a number of brief episodes. He appoints seventy missionaries to spread his word among all the nations, reminds a lawyer that love toward God and one's neighbors is the most important virtue, and explains that all those who act kindly, regardless of whether they are Jew or Gentile, are neighbors. He tells his disciples how they should pray, teaching them the Lord's Prayer and telling them that any sincere request will be granted by God. Jesus says, "Ask, and it will be given you" (11:9). He cautions extensively against ostentation and against the accumulation of wealth. Responding to attacks from the Pharisees, he accuses them of hypocrisy, for caring more about the letter of the law than about "justice and the love of God" (11:42). Perhaps anticipating further attacks by disbelievers, he tells his followers to be bold in asserting the Gospel's truth, and to be prepared for the unexpected final judgment. He works his way toward Jerusalem, delivering parables and lessons whose morals center around faith in God: the importance of repentance; the virtues of humility and kindness; the dangers of riches; the reward of total renunciation of the worldly in favor of the divine; and the ruin that will come to those who fail to listen to God's word.

Arriving in Jerusalem, Jesus foresees the destruction of the great city as a punishment for its failure to recognize him. Driving away the merchants, Jesus begins to preach in the temple and wins the allegiance of the common people. He refuses to justify his authority to the chief priests and elders who oppose him. Chastising them, he compares them to wicked tenants, who will be evicted and punished by the Lord, the true owner of the temple. The Jewish leaders attempt to entrap Jesus verbally, but he subverts them while asserting the importance of obedience to secular authority and belief in the resurrection of the dead. Jesus prophesies that the mighty temple will be destroyed and speaks of the great torment that will accompany the Apocalypse, preceding the End of Days and the return of the Son of man, one of Christ's titles.

Passover arrives, and Jesus celebrates the traditional Seder meal with his disciples. At the Seder, he institutes the Eucharist, the ritual consumption of wine and bread as symbols of Jesus's blood and body, signs of the new covenant. Jesus cautions his disciples not to fight about who among them is greatest, and reminds them that serving is greater than being served. He promises them rewards for their faithfulness. He also foretells that Simon Peter will falter in his faith. This prophecy proves true when, soon afterward, the chief priests and elders arrest Jesus, who has been betrayed by Judas Iscariot, one of the apostles. Peter, frightened, thrice denies all knowledge of Jesus. Brought before the Sanhedrin, the Jewish court, Jesus neither affirms nor denies his identity as God's son, answering questions with the simple statement, "You say that I am" (22:70). The court considers this statement a confession and brings him before the Roman prefect, Pilate. Pilate hesitates to convict Jesus, but the chief priests and elders eventually convince Pilate to sentence Jesus to death. Jesus is crucified, going to his death with the words, "Father, forgive them; for they do not know what they are doing," and is viciously mocked by the Roman guards (23:34). Joseph of Arimathea buries him.

On Sunday, the third day after Jesus's Friday crucifixion, some female followers of Jesus, including Mary Magdalene, go to his gravesite but find him gone. Angels appear and tell them that Jesus has been resurrected from the dead. The women tell the apostles what they have seen, but the apostles do not believe them. Peter goes to check the grave himself, and is amazed at not finding Jesus's body. Finally, Jesus appears to the dumbfounded disciples and gives them his last instructions: "in his name to all nations, beginning from Jerusalem. You are witnesses of these things" (24:47–48).

ANALYSIS

Although the Gospels of Matthew, Mark, and Luke tell basically the same story, there are important differences between the Gospels that help identify the special interests of each author. A comparison of the different genealogies of Jesus offers a good example. In Matthew's Gospel, Jesus's family lineage is traced back through important Jewish families, culminating with Abraham, the father of the Jewish people. This line of descent fits well with Matthew's emphasis on Jesus's continuity with the Old Testament and the Jewish people. In contrast, Luke's genealogy downplays Judaic roots and traces Jesus's parentage to Adam, the universal man of the Old Testament. Luke's emphasis on Jesus's common humanity gives scholars reason to think that Luke could have been a learned Gentile speaking to a largely Gentile audience. Although he may have been in a non-Jewish community, Luke was a meticulous historian and a learned man, who would have known some of the more widely circulating stories of the Jews, such as the story of Adam and Eve. Luke had to make sense of the fact that Jesus was indeed a Jew, and he would have been compelled to take into account some kind of Jewish heritage, so he chose to emphasize that which would be the most universal and inclusive of Gentiles. Likewise, other characteristics of Luke's account make comparatively few references to the Old Testament, which would have been strange and perhaps even unknown to his largely Gentile audience.

In the earliest parts of his Gospel, Luke tells many of the same miracle and healing stories contained in Mark, describing Jesus healing a leper, announcing the forgiveness of sins, and restoring life to the widow's son. Like Matthew, Luke deviates from Mark's Gospel and includes what he calls the Sermon on the Plain, which is Luke's equivalent to Matthew's description of the Sermon on the Mount. Luke is persistently concerned for the poor and the outcast, and his description of Jesus's sermon includes a series of warnings to the rich, fat, and mirthful (6:24–26). Chapter 7 introduces further incidents of Jesus's ministry in Galilee that are distinct from both Matthew and Mark and give us an indication of Luke's special interests: the faith of the Centurion's slave emphasizes and encourages the faith of a Gentile (7:1–10); the healing of the Widow's Son demonstrates Jesus's concern for a widow (7:11–17); the Ministering Woman in Chapter 8 stresses Jesus's readiness to help and be helped by women. Luke returns to Mark's Gospel for the subsequent miracles and healing stories.

The next Lucan section, "The Journey to Jerusalem," is the Gospel's longest, most loosely organized section (9.51–19:27). In this section, the narrative begins to move toward Jerusalem for the crucifixion, resurrection, and ascension—the ascension being the central event of Luke's Gospel. Contained in this section are some of the most well known parables in the entire New Testament, found only in Luke. These include the story of the Good Samaritan, a parable that reflects Luke's interest in Jesus's boundary-breaking behavior in associating with outcasts such as the Samaritans, a community once despised by Jews. Luke also includes a unique parable about Mary and Martha in which Jesus praises Mary, the female disciple who neglects her chores to listen to Jesus, and gently reproaches Martha, who is preoccupied by the traditional domestic duties of a woman. Also included are other well-known parables, such as those about the mustard seed and the rich fool storing his excess grain, and lessons on prayer, discipleship, and devotion—all of which stress the dangers of wealth and the importance of devotion to Jesus's way.

Chapter 15 is considered one of the greatest chapters of the New Testament. In it, Luke depicts three separate parables about being lost. The parable about the lost sheep among the ninety-nine found shows God's unending concern for the lost. The parable of the lost coin is similar, as is the famous story of the prodigal son, who is lost from his family and the standards of his father. The sheep, coin, and son are all found and returned to loving hands in their rightful places, which Luke uses to represent God's love and concern for the lost and forgotten. The loving concern exhibited toward these characters reflects the concern shown by Jesus, which the disciple must strive to emulate.

At a time in which most women were excluded from participating in public life in Rome, and were considered ritually impure for a substantial portion of their life according to Jewish custom, Luke's special concern for women and other outcasts of society is truly remarkable. His concern gives historians reason to think that there must have been a significant number of prominent female converts in Luke's community. Luke praises the courage of Mary, who rejoices over her fate to conceive the Son of God. From Luke, we also learn a bit more about Mary Magdalene, one of Jesus's closest disciples, who follows him to the tomb and is among the first to see that Jesus's body is missing. Luke tells us that Mary Magdalene was just one of many woman who travels with Jesus and his male disciples in an age when the mixing of sexes was virtually unheard of. Luke also tells us that these courageous women "provided for them out of their resources" (8:3). In other words, women in the Gospel of Luke are largely responsible for the finances of Jesus's followers. In Acts, Luke describes Lydia, the wealthy merchant who provides for Paul, along with Pricilla, Aquila, and Philip's four daughters, who are prophetesses (21:9).

Along with his concern and esteem for women, Luke also shows preferential concern for the poor and the outcast. He repeatedly insists on the dangers of wealth and "abundance of possessions," but blesses and esteems those who are in fact impoverished (12:15). These words must have been shocking to urban Gentile ears in a society in which the overwhelming majority of the population was destitute, impoverished, and enslaved—but now, suddenly, according to Jesus, blessed. While Luke takes great risks in his patriarchal, hierarchical, and divisive society with his shocking words of inclusion and universalism, he also makes concessions. Luke's Gospel and Acts of the Apostles are the most pro-Roman works of the New Testament. Luke is insistent on maintaining Pontius Pilate's innocence in the crucifixion of the Jews and places all guilt in the hands of the Jewish leaders. In Acts, during the stoning of Stephen, Stephen says to a violent Jewish mob in Jerusalem, "You stiff-necked people, uncircumcised in heart and ears, you are forever opposing the Holy Spirit, just as your ancestors used to do. Which of the prophets did your ancestors not persecute? They killed those who foretold the coming of the Righteous One, and now you have become his betrayers and murderers" (Acts 7:51–52).

Such loaded rhetoric is generally viewed as Luke's attempt to persuade the Roman officials that the Christian Church, rapidly growing in Gentile converts, was no threat to the Roman Empire. This minority community wanted to appear on the side of the Romans so as to give the empire, whose disregard for human life has been nearly unrivaled in world history, no reason to pay them any heed or to regard them as a threat. The stories in Luke and Acts are politically structured to put all blame on the Jews, who were already a suspicious group with an alternative lifestyle to that of the Greco-Roman Empire, with its Greek philosophy and Roman Gods. This finger-pointing has indicated to historians that by the time of Luke, Christianity had become much more Gentile and less Jewish in its identity.

THE GOSPEL ACCORDING TO JOHN (JOHN)

INTRODUCTION

> *In the beginning was the Word, and the Word was with God, and the Word was God. He was in the beginning with God.*
>
> *(See* QUOTATIONS, *p. 66)*

The Fourth Gospel describes the mystery of the identity of Jesus. The Gospel According to John develops a Christology—an explanation of Christ's nature and origin—while leaving out much of the familiar material that runs through the synoptic Gospels of Matthew, Mark and Luke, including Jesus's short aphorisms and parables, references to Jesus's background, and proclamations about the kingdom of God. Whereas Mark's Gospel brings us the texture of first-century Palestine with a vivid, concrete, and earthy Jesus, John's Gospel is filled with long discourses describing Jesus's divinity. John takes us behind Jesus's ministry, where we get a glimpse of what it means to believe in Jesus as flesh of the eternal and living God, as the source of light and life, and for a believer to be a "Son of God." Though John's narrative diverges from the synoptic Gospels, it is indeed a Gospel, or a telling of good news. It includes the basics of Jesus's ministry—his preaching, miracles, trial, crucifixion, and resurrection. It is likely that John heard the details about these events from a very early oral source common to all the Gospels, but the freedom he uses to interpret these events helps us see clearly that all accounts of Jesus have come to us through the filter of interpretation. John may have been written a bit later than the synoptic Gospels, likely around 90 A.D. The actual author of

John's Gospel was probably an interpreter of John, who was one of Jesus's original disciples.

John can be divided thematically into halves, preceded by a prologue and followed by an epilogue. The prologue is a poetic introduction that presents the outline of the narrative and the essence of John's theology. The first half of the Gospel can be characterized as a "Book of Signs." It tells of Jesus's ministry, focusing on seven major miracles worked by Jesus and the meaning and significance of those miracles. The second half of John has been called the "Book of Glory." In it, the narrative moves toward Jesus's glorification through crucifixion and resurrection. Finally, the book ends with an epilogue, most likely added to the Gospel by a later redactor, which tells of Jesus's appearance to the disciples after his resurrection.

SUMMARY

The Gospel of John begins with a poetic hymn that tells the story of Jesus's origin, mission, and function. John says that Jesus is the incarnated Word of God, bringing "grace and truth," replacing the law given by Moses, and making God known in the world (1:17). The narrative opens with John the Baptist identifying himself as the fulfillment of Isaiah's prophecy; he will prepare the way for the Lord. Indeed, when he meets Jesus, John testifies, "He is the Son of God" (1:34). The next day, hearing John's testimony, two disciples, including Andrew, begin to follow Jesus. Andrew brings his brother Simon to Jesus, who now accumulates several other followers as well. On the third day after Jesus's baptism, Jesus and his disciples attend a wedding at Cana in Galilee, where Jesus works a miracle, transforming water into wine. As Passover approaches, Jesus travels to Jerusalem, where he drives the money changers from the temple, charging them to "stop making my Father's house a marketplace" (2:16). A Pharisee named Nicodemus assumes that Jesus has come from God as a teacher, and Jesus tells him, in solemn, semipoetic lines, that he has been "born from above" (3:3) and that God has given "his only Son so that everyone who believes in him may not perish" (3:16). Jesus leaves Jerusalem and begins to baptize people in Judea. John the Baptist has continued his baptizing, and someone informs him that Jesus too has begun to baptize, assuming that John would be angry at the competition. The Baptist rejoices at the news, knowing that Jesus, as the Son of God, is the greater of the two, and that Jesus is the fulfillment of John's prophecy.

Jesus travels to Samaria, where he speaks in metaphors and figures of speech with a Samaritan woman and with his disciples. They do not always understand his metaphors, and take Jesus literally when he tells the woman that he has "living water" (4:10) and when he tells his disciples that "I have food to eat that you do not know about" (4:32). Eventually, the woman understands Jesus. Impressed by his knowledge of her past and by his message, she tells the other Samaritans that he is the Christ, meaning that he is the Messiah prophesied in Jewish scriptures. The Samaritans profess belief in him. Returning to Cana in Galilee, Jesus cures a boy who is at death's door. In Jerusalem once again for a festival, Jesus cures a sick man at the pool of Bethzatha and orders him to pick up his sleeping mat and walk around. As it is the Sabbath, when observant Jews do not carry objects outdoors, the Jews become angry with Jesus, and their anger only increases when Jesus explains that God is his father. Jesus delivers a long discourse, in which he announces that his words bring eternal life, and that rejection of Jesus in favor of the traditional laws is foolish, since Jesus represents the fulfillment of the Old Testament prophecies.

Returning to Galilee, Jesus is approached by a crowd of people looking for inspiration. To feed them, he works a miracle, providing food for 5,000 people with only five loaves of bread and two fish. Later that evening, Jesus's disciples are crossing the Sea of Galilee and are surprised to find Jesus walking across the water toward them. The next day, crowds of people come in search of Jesus, and he explains the significance of the miracle of the loaves: "I am the bread of life / no one can come to me unless it is granted by the Father" (6:35). Using the symbol of bread, Jesus explains that belief in him and in God, his father, will give eternal life. Many of his listeners disbelieve him, and Jesus teaches that belief in him is a fore-ordained gift from God: "Do not judge by appearances, but judge with right judgment" (6:65). Peter, however, remains with Jesus and professes his faith.

At the Feast of Booths, the Jewish holiday Sukkoth, Jesus returns to Jerusalem with the pilgrims and begins preaching in the temple. He urges the people not to hold his previous violation of the Sabbath against him, saying, "Do not judge by appearances, but judge with right judgment" (7:24). Many people wonder whether Jesus is the Christ, or Son of God, and the authorities want to arrest him but do not dare. The authorities bring him an adulterous woman and, in an attempt to entrap him, ask him whether or not she is guilty. Jesus responds, "Let anyone among you who is without sin be the first to throw a stone at her" (8:7). A long discourse ensues, in which Jesus responds to questions and accusations from the assembled people. Jesus predicts his own death and ascension, and explains that his authority comes from his origin in God and his fulfillment of the word of God. He accuses his listeners of being slaves to sin and, as sinners, of being illegitimate sons of God. Claiming to precede Abraham and to derive his glory from God, Jesus finally infuriates the crowd and barely escapes being stoned.

Jesus comes upon a man blind from birth and gives the man sight. The Pharisees are frustrated to realize that Jesus really has cured the man, who now professes faith in him. For their failure to believe, Jesus pronounces the Pharisees blind and teaches that he is the good shepherd, and that it is only through him that the sheep of Israel's flock shall be saved. Months pass, and at the Feast of Dedication, the Jewish holiday Hanukkah, Jesus is again confronted by the Jews in the temple, who ask whether or not he is the Christ. He responds by announcing that he is the Son of God, united with God. The crowd tries to stone him, but Jesus escapes Jerusalem.

Jesus is called to Bethany, the village where two of his devout followers, Mary and Martha, live with their brother Lazarus, who has fallen sick. Arriving in Bethany too late, Jesus finds Lazarus dead. He works a miracle to inspire belief in the observers, resurrecting Lazarus. Hearing of this spectacle, the Jewish leadership in Jerusalem, including the chief priests, decides to kill both Jesus and Lazarus. Nevertheless, Jesus travels to Jerusalem for Passover. He has foreseen his own death, as well as the salvation that he will bring through his sacrifice. Many of the Jews, despite witnessing signs of Jesus's divinity, continue to disbelieve, and Jesus decries their lack of faith.

At the Passover meal, or Seder, Jesus preaches extensively to the apostles. Through washing their feet, he teaches them that they must serve each other, saying, "I give you a new commandment, that you love one another" (13:34). Jesus stresses his unity with God: "I am in the Father, and the Father is in me" (14:10). Jesus foresees his own death and his betrayal by Judas. "I am going to the Father," he tells the apostles (14:28). Jesus assures the apostles that in Jesus's place, God will send an advocate, the Spirit of God, who will continue to dwell with the faithful, and who will lead them toward truth and salvation. He warns them that even after his death, they will continue to be persecuted, but that their ultimate salvation is imminent.

Hearing this prophesy, the apostles finally express their firm belief in Jesus, and Jesus responds triumphantly, "I have conquered the world" (16:33). In a long, private prayer, Jesus addresses God directly, asking him to consecrate, glorify, and protect the faithful.

The narrative moves quickly toward its conclusion. Jesus is arrested by the soldiers whom Judas leads to him. He is brought first before the Jewish high priest, and then before Pontius Pilate, the Roman prefect. Pilate repeatedly interrogates Jesus, who refuses to confirm the allegation against him—that he has acted treasonably against Caesar by declaring himself King of the Jews. Pilate is reluctant to condemn Jesus, but the Jews agitate for Jesus's execution, and eventually Pilate consents. Jesus is crucified, and the soldiers cast lots to determine who will get his clothing. Pilate affixes a notice to the cross, reading "Jesus of Nazareth the King of the Jews" (19:19). Jesus dies, and to ensure his death, a solider pierces his side with a lance. Joseph of Arimathea and Nicodemus bury Jesus on a Friday.

On Sunday morning, Mary Magdalene comes to Jesus's grave and finds it empty. Jesus appears to her, and she brings the news of his resurrection to the disciples. Later that day, he appears to the disciples, whom he charges with the propagation of his message: "As the Father has sent me, so I send you" (20:21). Thomas is absent from the room, and he expresses doubt as to the resurrection until, a week later, Jesus reappears to him as well.

> For I have set you an example that you also should do as I have done to you.
>
> (See QUOTATIONS, p. 69)

ANALYSIS

For John, Jesus's miracles are not simply wonders to astonish onlookers, but signs pointing to his glory that come from the presence of God within him. In the early stages of his ministry, John tells of an encounter between Jesus and a Samaritan woman at the well. At this time, the Samaritans were a group of people despised by the Jews, and casual conversation between men and women was taboo. Jesus asks the woman to fetch him water, but she misunderstands his words to mean literal water. Quickly, she learns that the water to which he refers is already in her presence, that Jesus is "a spring of water gushing up to eternal life," to which she replies, "Sir, give me this water so that I may never be thirsty" (4:14-15). This story is not a short parable, but an opportunity for Jesus to explain elaborately his personhood using life giving symbols characteristic of John's writing: water, words, bread, and light. John tells of this Samaritan woman leaving to then become a successful missionary of the "good news" in Samaria (4:42).

All the Gospel narratives diverge dramatically after the point at which Mark ends: the discovery of the empty tomb and the astonishment of the women. In Matthew, the women run to tell the disciples and are met by the risen Jesus on the way. In Luke, the women tell of their discovery of an empty tomb, but no one believes them until the resurrected Jesus makes a series of appearances before the other disciples. Here, in John's Gospel, Mary Magdalene tells Peter and another disciple of the empty tomb, and, though she first mistakes him for a gardener, Jesus appears to her and discloses his identity. After his appearance to Mary, the risen Jesus appears to the disciples as a group, and John dramatizes the spiritual presence of Christ when Jesus breathes on his disciples. In both Hebrew and Greek, the word for "breath" is the same as that for "spirit."

The Gospel of John is perhaps the most difficult of the Gospels to understand, not because John is more complex than the others—Luke is perhaps the most technically difficult of the Gospels—but because it is so different from the other Gospels. Reading John in the context of the other Gospels can be a jarring experience, because the theological significance of the picture that John paints of Jesus's life is in many respects specific to John himself. Even John's solemn and poetic presentation is quite different from that of the other Gospels. The Gospel is also resistant to ecumenicalism, or attempts to reconcile varying religions; in the Gospel of John, Jesus declares, "I am the way, and the truth, and the life, No one comes to the Father except through me" (14:16).

Yet the Gospel of John also contains some of the most beautiful parts of the New Testament, such as Jesus's statement, "Let anyone among you who is without sin be the first to throw a stone at her" (8:7). Scholars believe that this story was circulating orally, and that church leaders were reluctant to add it into any of the synoptic Gospels because in official church doctrine, forgiveness for adultery was impossible. Instead of focusing on an official church, John's Gospel focuses on individual believers and their relationships to Jesus.

Perhaps the most striking aspect of John is its development of Christology, a discourse on the nature and origin of Jesus. Unlike Matthew and Luke, John is not interested in the details of Jesus's birth. Both Matthew and Luke stress that Jesus is born of a human mother who has somehow been visited by the Holy Spirit. John skips entirely the question of Jesus's conception. In fact, taken by itself, John offers no indication of any supernatural birth. Instead, John pictures Jesus as the Son of God in a sense that might be described as metaphorical. Jesus may well be a real human who possesses flesh and blood, but he is also the incarnation of the Divine Word. Indeed, just as Jesus himself is the Son of God, John speaks of Jesus giving his followers "power to become children of God"—descent from God is an attitude of faith and a gift of grace (1:12).

ACTS OF THE APOSTLES (ACTS)

INTRODUCTION

Acts of the Apostles, the second part of the work that begins with the Gospel According to Luke, is the story of the early church after Jesus's martyrdom. Like Luke, Acts is addressed to the unknown reader Theophilus, and in the introduction to Acts, it is made clear that it is a continuation of Luke: "In the first book, Theophilus, I wrote about all that Jesus did and taught from the beginning until the day he was taken up to heaven" (1:1–2). Second-century Christian tradition identifies the author of Luke and Acts as Luke, a traveling companion of the missionary Paul of Tarsus. Modern scholars agree that Acts and Luke should be credited to the same author, but have been more reluctant to identify him: the author most likely wrote between the years 80 and 90, and may indeed have been Paul's companion.

One of the perplexing problems surrounding the authorship of Acts is the narrator's changing voice and person. He generally speaks as an uninvolved third party, but sometimes lapses into the plural. Acts is certainly intended as a history of the early church, and it is the most complete and valuable history we have of the Christians in the first century. However, it is not necessarily historically reliable, either in terms of its depiction of the first-century development of Christian theology and religion, or in its description of the political history of the church. For instance, the author seems relatively shaky in his knowledge of Paul's theology. Whether or not it was intended to be a historically accurate text, Acts can be read as a devotional and instructional history, whose religious purpose remains unaffected by its inaccuracies. It depicts the story of the spread of Christianity, the growing distance between Christianity and Judaism, the move toward earthly concerns rather than

SUMMARY & ANALYSIS

apocalyptic expectations, and the triumph of the Christian message despite persecutions.

SUMMARY

Acts begins with Jesus's charge to the Twelve Apostles to spread the Gospel throughout the world. Peter serves as the leader of the apostles and the small congregation of the faithful in Jerusalem. Their first order of business is to elect Matthias as the twelfth apostle, replacing the traitor Judas Iscariot. During the year of Jesus's death and resurrection, the disciples are gathered for Pentecost, a religious holiday celebrating the grain harvest. The Holy Spirit descends upon them. As a result of the Holy Spirit's presence, they begin speaking other languages.

Peter delivers a sermon explaining the miracle. He says that the gift of tongues is given to prophets. Peter summarizes the life, crucifixion, and resurrection of Jesus. He gives scriptural proof that Jesus is the Messiah, the savior whom God promises in the Old Testament to send to save Jews from their adversity. Responding to Peter's sermon, 3,000 people are baptized into the Christian community—an idealized, thriving community characterized by prayer, brotherhood, common ownership, and sharing. A man named Barnabas is particularly praised for his generosity, and a couple that defrauds the church is stricken dead. Going to the temple to pray, Peter and John cure a crippled beggar. Peter tells a crowd the story of Jesus's persecution and his eventual resurrection, concluding with a reminder that the Jews are favored by God and a call to repentance. The Sadducee high priests of the temple, who do not believe in the resurrection of the dead, bring Peter and John before the Jewish high court, where Peter preaches the Gospel fearlessly. The court, which is called the Sanhedrin, recognizes that public opinion is in favor of the apostles and releases them with only a warning.

The high priest imprisons the apostles, but they are miraculously freed by an angel, and they continue their preaching. Brought again before the court, Peter leads the apostles in their defense, saying, "We must obey God rather than any human authority" (5:29). Influenced by the great sage Gamaliel, who warns, "[Y]ou will not be able to overthrow them—in that case you may even be found fighting against God," the court declines to execute the apostles, who continue preaching throughout Jerusalem (5:39).

The church divides into two groups. One group is the Hellenists, Christians who were born Jewish but who have a Greek cultural background. The other group is the Hebrews, the Christians who, like the apostles, were born into Jewish cultural backgrounds. The Hellenists feel discriminated against, so in response, the community of disciples elects seven leaders to account for the needs of the Hellenists. Foremost among these Christian Hellenist leaders is Stephen. A controversy ensues between Stephen and some Jews, who accuse him of heresy before the Sanhedrin. Stephen's accusers testify that "[t]his man never stops saying things against the holy place and the law" (7:13). In front of the Sanhedrin, Stephen delivers a long speech detailing the history of Jewish leadership in the Bible, concluding with a damning accusation: "Yet the Most High does not dwell in houses made with human hands. . . . You stiff-necked people . . . you are forever opposing the Holy Spirit, just as your ancestors used to do" (7:48–51).

Stephen is stoned to death, with the approval of a young man named Saul of Damascus, a vigorous persecutor of the Christians. Stephen is the first Christian martyr, a person who is killed as a result of defending the church. Saul is a Jewish leader who has been trying to wipe out the new community of Christians because he believes that they are trying to dismantle Jewish law. While traveling to persecute Christians, Saul is blinded by a light and hears the voice of Jesus asking, "Saul, Saul why do you persecute me?" (Acts 9:4). Saul then sets out to become the most relentless, brilliant, and bold missionary of Christianity that the church has ever known. He travels to the coast, performs miracles, preaches the Gospel, and converts Gentiles.

In a brief interlude, Acts recounts the miracles and speeches of Peter. Traveling to the coast, Peter cures a paralytic at Lydda and revives a woman at Joppa. In Caesarea, he says that he has received a message from God telling him that he "should not call anyone profane or unclean" (10:28). He deduces that he may associate with Gentiles, as "God shows no partiality, but in every nation anyone who fears him and does what is right is acceptable to him" (10:34). He therefore dines with the family of a Roman centurion named Cornelius, and they become the first Gentiles baptized by Peter. The church continues to shift its emphasis toward welcoming the Gentiles. Some of those who fled persecutions in Jerusalem arrive at the Syrian city of Antioch, where they begin to preach to the Greeks. Saul and Barnabas are among these people. Judea, meanwhile, is under the rule of King Herod Agrippa, who ruled from 41 to 44 A.D. Herod Agrippa introduces institutional persecution against the

Christians and arrests Peter, who is miraculously freed from jail by an angel.

Barnabas and Saul, who is renamed Paul, depart on a missionary journey. In Cyprus, Paul blinds a magician, Elymas, who tries to prevent Paul from teaching. At Antioch in Pisidia, a central region in modern-day Turkey, Paul preaches to a Jewish congregation, telling his listeners about forgiveness of sins through faith in Jesus as the resurrected Messiah. Many listeners become converts, but many also contradict Paul, and the missionaries are expelled from the territory. At Iconium, too, they have some success until nonbelievers, including both Jews and Gentiles, drive them from town. At Lycaonia, Paul cures a cripple, and the local Gentiles take them for the pagan gods Zeus and Hermes before Paul is able to convince them otherwise. As usual, however, the missionaries are chased from town, and Paul is nearly stoned to death. The two make their way back to Antioch in Syria, preaching the whole way. A controversy arises as a result of their missionary activities among the Gentiles, and Paul and Barnabas journey to Jerusalem for a debate of church leaders.

At the debate, traditional Jewish Christians argue that, to become a Christian, one must first convert to Judaism and become circumcised. Paul and Barnabas are strong supporters of expanding the church among Gentiles. Peter and James, leaders of the Jewish Christians in Jerusalem, decide in favor of Paul's perspective, arguing that they should preserve the community of believers and "not trouble those Gentiles who are turning to God" (15:19). Only a minimal adherence to the law is required of Christian Gentiles. Paul separates from Barnabas and, together with another disciple, Silas, sets out in Macedonia. Local Gentiles are angry at their exorcism of a spirit from a soothsayer slave, which deprives her of the ability to tell the future. They imprison Paul and Silas. An earthquake shakes the prison cell, and the missionaries are quickly released.

In Greece, Paul meets with mixed success, converting some but meeting opposition from many Jews and some Gentiles. In Athens, Paul speaks at the public forum, the Areopagus, contextualizing Christianity within Greek beliefs. From Athens, Paul travels to Corinth, where he turns away from the Jews in despair and preaches almost entirely to the Gentiles with great success. He also attracts his faithful disciples Aquila and Priscilla. The Jews take Paul before the governor of the region to accuse him, but the governor refuses to adjudicate a matter of religious faith. Paul, after a brief return to

Antioch, continues to work his way through Greece, establishing the church in Ephesus and working great miracles. He leaves Ephesus after a mass riot instigated by the silversmiths, who are concerned that Paul's preaching against pagan idolatry will ruin their trade.

Paul travels onward and stops to revive a dead man in Troas. Paul sends for the Christian elders of Ephesus, and in an emotional speech he reminds them of his faithful service to them and warns them of the persecution that might begin. The Holy Spirit urges him to travel to Jerusalem, where he himself expects to be persecuted and possibly killed. In Jerusalem, Paul meets with James and the church leaders, who are concerned that Paul appears to have been urging Christians not to follow Jewish law. They plan for Paul to make a public show of worship at the temple, to indicate that he continues to adhere to Jewish law. In the temple, however, Jews seize him, accusing him of profaning the temple and preaching against the law. Paul tells the crowd his personal history. He relates the stories of his past persecution of Christians, his miraculous vision of Christ, and his conversion to Christianity and mission to preach to the Gentiles.

The crowd becomes outraged, and the Roman tribune seizes Paul and flogs him. The tribune then has him brought before the Jewish high court, the Sanhedrin, where Paul creates dissent by setting the two factions in the court, the Pharisees and the Sadducees, against each other. The tribune saves Paul from the ensuing riot, and, hearing of a Jewish plot against Paul's life, sends him for his own protection to Felix, the governor of Palestine, in Caesarea. At the trial in Caesarea, Paul professes to worship God and adhere to Jewish law. He claims that it is only because of his belief in the resurrection of the dead—a belief not shared by the Sadducees—that he is on trial. Hearing that Paul collects and distributes alms, Felix holds him in jail for two years, hoping for a bribe. After Felix's death, Paul is tried before the new governor, Festus. Paul appeals to Caesar's judgment, and Festus—who does not believe Paul guilty, but who wants to appease the Jews calling for his execution—resolves to send him to Caesar, in Rome. First, however, Paul is brought before Herod Agrippa, the Jewish puppet-king of Palestine. Again, Paul recounts the story of his vision of Jesus and conversion to Christianity, and argues that his missionary activity is merely a fulfillment of Jewish hopes and Old Testament prophecies. King Herod Agrippa is impressed, but Paul is sent to Rome. On the way to Rome, Paul's ship is wrecked, and through a series of sailing mishaps it takes months to arrive at Rome. Awaiting his hearing at Rome, Paul begins to spread the Gospel to the Roman Jews, who disbelieve him. He turns his emphasis again toward the Gentiles, and as Acts ends, Paul is in Rome, "teaching about the Lord Jesus Christ with all boldness and without hindrance" (28:31).

ANALYSIS

Acts of the Apostles demonstrates the importance of missionary work in the early church. The book begins with the appearance of the resurrected Jesus to his disciples, who are anxious for the final redemption. The apostles demand of Jesus, "Lord, is this the time when you will restore the kingdom to Israel?" (1:6). Jesus responds by charging them to concern themselves not with the Apocalypse, but with spreading the Gospel on Earth: "It is not for you to know the times or periods that the Father has set by his own authority. But you will receive power when the Holy Spirit has come upon you; and you will be my witnesses in Jerusalem, and in all Judea and Samaria, and to the ends of the earth" (1:7–8). It is through Paul, the great early missionary of the church, that Acts dramatizes the fulfillment of Jesus's command, the spreading of the Gospel across the known world. Paul dominates the second half of Acts and, more than any other figure, dictates the trajectory of the church's rise. Acts begins with Peter and the apostles in Jerusalem; it ends, years later, with Paul in Rome. Paul's final words are an apt summary of the direction in which he leads the missionary church in the vital first decades of its existence: "Let it be known to you then," he says to the Jews of Rome, "that this salvation of God has been sent to the Gentiles; they will listen" (28:28).

The ending of Acts in Rome foreshadows the eventual transition of the church to that city. Acts is the story of the church's turn away from Jerusalem and toward Antioch, Ephesus, and Rome. Acts is filled with stories and speeches, but the dramatic arc that connects all of Acts of the Apostles is the church's move, driven by Paul, toward a split with Judaism and an emphasis on converting Gentiles. It is in that move that Christianity becomes its own distinct religion. Jesus and his followers consider themselves Jews, and Jesus's message and teachings are the fulfillment of Jewish prophecies. It is evident from the first chapters of Acts that, in the first years after Jesus's ascension, the apostles and their followers continued to consider themselves Jews, and to follow Jewish law. Peter and John, both of whom consider Jews the chosen people of God, are on their way to worship in the Jewish temple when they encounter the cripple. "You are the descendents of the prophets," Peter tells a Jewish audience, "and of the covenant that God gave to your ancestors. . . . When God raised up his servant [Jesus], he sent him first to you" (3:25–26).

The early church controversy between the Hellenists and the Hebrews introduces the first dissent within the church itself. The Hellenists are Jewish adherents to Jesus who were born into a Greek cultural background. They feel that the Hebrews, Jewish Christians who were born into a Jewish cultural background and who adhere strictly to Jewish law, are discriminating against them. The apostles and disciples decide that unity is more important than conformity, and they accept the position of the Hellenists, even appointing Stephen and six others to minister to the Hellenists in the church. When Stephen breaks with Jewish tradition, however, he shows how Christianity is becoming increasingly incompatible with Judaism. Although Stephen is stoned to death, the Hellenists continue to move away from the Jewish focus of the church, baptizing Samaritans and an Ethiopian. A turning point for the church occurs when Peter himself receives a message from God: "God has shown me that I must not call anyone profane or unclean" (10:28). The message challenges one of the fundamental aspects of Judaism, the idea that Jews are a special population chosen by God. But God's message to Peter indicates that Gentiles are no less clean than Jews, and therefore that "God has given even to the Gentiles the repentance that leads to life" (11:18).

The church in Antioch is founded immediately after the Jerusalem elders accept Peter's rationale for baptizing a Gentile, thus laying the foundation for the Antioch church to become dominated by Gentile Christians. It also indicates the increasing degree to which followers of Jesus Christ are non-Jewish. The acceptance of Gentiles gives impetus to the move away from Jewish law and Judaism, and it signals the beginning of the move away from Jerusalem. In fact, at Antioch the disciples are first called Christians rather than Jews. Paul becomes the great Christian missionary to the Gentiles, traveling throughout Greece and Asia Minor and, while receiving little welcome from the Jews, recruiting many Gentiles to the church. Paul and Barnabus say, "It was necessary that the word of God should be spoken first to you. Since you reject it and judge yourselves to be unworthy of eternal life, we are now turning to the Gentiles" (13:46).

SUMMARY & ANALYSIS

The New Testament texts are not monolithic, or conveying only a single, objective perspective. The Book of Acts reveals that early Christianity was a highly dynamic movement, full of doctrinal and theological differences. Acts functions as a historical text in allowing us a unique insight into the transition of Christianity from a Jewish sect into its own religion. The controversies over adherence to Jewish law, the role of Gentiles within the church, and the relationship of the Diaspora communities to the Jerusalem community make it possible to understand Paul's letters, which comprise a later part of the New Testament. Acts describes the beginning of the process by which the faith of a few followers grew into a church that dominated Europe for more than 1,000 years.

THE LETTER OF PAUL TO THE ROMANS (ROMANS)

INTRODUCTION

Of the twenty-seven books in the New Testament, fourteen have traditionally been attributed to the great missionary Paul of Tarsus. These fourteen books all take the form of letters addressed to a given individual or community. In the traditional canonical ordering of the New Testament, these fourteen books are arranged in a block following Acts, and separated into three groups: the nine letters addressed to communities, the four letters addressed to individuals, and Hebrews. Within each grouping, the traditional canonical system orders the books according to length. Thus, a traditional New Testament arrangement will list the books as follows: Romans, 1 and 2 Corinthians, Galatians, Ephesians, Philippians, Colossians, 1 and 2 Thessalonians, 1 and 2 Timothy, Titus, Philemon, and Hebrews. This SparkNote addresses only a few of the most important letters: Romans, 1 and 2 Corinthians, and Ephesians. Modern scholars agree with the traditional second-century Christian belief that seven of these New Testament letters were almost certainly written by Paul himself: 1 Thessalonians, Galatians, Philippians, Philemon, 1 and 2 Corinthians, and Romans. These letters were most likely written during the height of Paul's missionary activity, between 50 and 58 A.D., making them the earliest surviving Christian documents—they predate the earliest of the Gospels, Mark, by at least ten years.

During the winter of 57–58 A.D., Paul was in the Greek city of Corinth. From Corinth, he wrote the longest single letter in the New

Testament, which he addressed to "God's beloved in Rome" (1:7). Like most New Testament letters, this letter is known by the name of the recipients, the Romans. Paul's letters tended to be written in response to specific crises. For instance, 1 Corinthians was written to reprove the Christian community in Corinth for its internal divisions and for its immoral sexual practices. But Romans is remarkably devoid of this kind of specificity, addressing broad questions of theology rather than specific questions of contemporary practice. Whereas other Pauline letters—2 Corinthians, for instance—are full of impassioned rhetoric and personal pleas, Romans is written in a solemn and restrained tone. Perhaps this solemnity can be explained by timing: Romans was the last written of the seven New Testament letters that modern scholars attribute to Paul, and has been seen as a summary of Paul's thought, composed as his career moved toward its conclusion. But it is also true that, as opposed to the Corinthian church, the Roman church was not founded by Paul himself. At the time when he wrote Romans, Paul had never visited Rome, although Chapter 16 of Romans does indicate that he had acquaintances there. Writing to a community largely composed of strangers, then, Paul may have felt compelled to use the restrained and magisterial declarations of Roman style, rather than the impassioned pleas and parental sternness that permeate his letters to the churches at Corinth.

Summary

Because he is not personally familiar with the Roman church, Paul begins his letter by introducing himself. He has been "called to be an apostle," and his mission is "to bring about the obedience of faith among all the Gentiles" (1:1–5). Paul follows his introduction with a flattering greeting to the Roman church, and expresses his desire to preach in Rome someday. Paul gives a summary of the theme of his letter: "The Gospel . . . is the power of God for salvation to everyone who has faith, to the Jew first and also to the Greek. For in it the righteousness of God is revealed through faith for faith" (1:16–17).

Paul begins with a discussion of the state of humanity before the possibility of salvation through faith in Jesus. He tells how Gentiles worshipped idols, disdaining devotion to God, and how Jews failed to follow the law properly, acting hypocritically by proclaiming allegiance to Jewish law while surreptitiously sinning. Paul says that God's ancestral promise to the Jews, symbolized by circumcision, does not bring automatic salvation: "A person is a Jew who is one inwardly, and real circumcision is a matter of the heart—it is spiritual" (2:29). Paul concludes, "We have already charged that all, both Jews and Greeks, are under the power of sin" (3:9).

Paul teaches that salvation from sin is only possible through faith. Paul cites the example of the biblical patriarch Abraham, who received God's blessing and passed it on to his descendents through "the righteousness of faith" (4:13). The free gift of grace, Paul continues, unearned and undeserved, is a product of God's love manifested toward the unworthy. Whereas Adam's fall brought sin and death into the world, Jesus's sacrifice brought grace and life. The importance of baptism, Paul explains, is that baptism initiates a new life of grace and purity: the sinner symbolically dies, baptized into the death of Jesus, and the person who emerges is "dead to sin and alive to God in Christ Jesus" (6:11). Christians, then, must be governed by holiness, not by sin: holiness alone will lead to eternal life. Jewish law ceases to be binding: the law arouses sinful passions, and as beings dead to sin, Christians become dead to the law. Paul urges the Romans to live not "according to the flesh" but rather by the Spirit (8:4). Through the Spirit, all believers become spiritual children of God, called by God to glory. This potential is a source of strength for the Christian: "If God is for us, who is against us?" (8:31).

Paul's next topic is the problem of reconciling the doctrine of salvation through faith in Christ with the Old Testament promise of the salvation of the Jewish people. This section begins with a lamentation, as Paul, who was himself born a Jew, expresses his wish to help the Israelites, the supposed firstborn children of God. But he goes on to explain that the Christian covenant of grace is by no means a betrayal of Abraham's covenant with God. Those who have faith in Jesus, who believe "with the heart," are "children of the promise," the spiritual children of Israel (10:10, 9:8). The genetic children of Israel, the Jews, stumbled when they mistook Jewish law for the means to salvation. But the Jews have not been entirely cast aside. Paul teaches that eventually the Jews will come to express faith in Jesus, enabling God to keep his original promise to them.

Finished with his exposition of Christian doctrine, Paul embarks upon a lengthy exhortation to the Romans, advising them on the proper means of living a Christian life. Harmony, humility, and love are his main concerns. He urges charity, forbearance, and submission. Paul returns to the apocalyptic theme on which he dwells in his other letters. He says that it is doubly important to act righteously in an apocalyptic age. In a long segment, Paul mandates tolerance and freedom of religious conscience within the church. The strong in faith are not to judge and reject the weak in faith—that is, those who have given up Jewish law are to accept the observances of those who continue to practice Jewish law. Paul finishes this section with a set of Old Testament quotations about the worship of God spreading among all nations. Paul concludes his letter with a section in which he discusses his own ministry, proving his authority through a discussion of his credentials: "I have reason to boast of my work for God" (15:17). He informs the Romans that he is preparing to bring the contributions of the Greek and Macedonian churches to Jerusalem, where he speculates that he might run into difficulties. Chapter 16 contains a long list of greetings, which many scholars believe were added by a later editor. Paul sends the greetings to the Roman Christians, warning the Romans to be wary of "those who cause dissensions and offenses" (16:17).

ANALYSIS

The period during which Paul wrote his letters was traumatic for the new church. Christianity had not yet evolved into a distinct religion with a hierarchy of authority and a defined dogma. Christianity, in its earliest years, was an offshoot of Judaism. Believers in Jesus, including all of the Twelve Apostles, were generally born Jewish and identified themselves as Jews who believed that the Old Testament prophecies had reached their fulfillment in Jesus. Indeed, the term "Christians" did not appear until Paul's ministry at Antioch, decades after Jesus's crucifixion. The church was not a single, unified body governed by a central authority, but, rather, a conglomeration of individual communities, often separated by large distances, which depended for spiritual authority on local preachers or traveling missionaries, like Paul. Christians in the decades after Jesus lived in constant fear of persecution and constant expectation of the second coming, Jesus's triumphant return to Earth during which he would save the faithful.

The letters that Paul wrote respond to these conditions of the early church. He addresses them to specific communities, most of which had been established by Paul himself. In an era when travel was slow and long-distance communication was difficult, Paul's letters were a means of preserving his spirit in a community once he had left, or of instructing a community from a distance. The aim of the letters was to inspire unity among believers and to instruct the faithful on difficult points of doctrine. The letters are highly individualized, responding to the specific problems of the community to which they are addressed. By and large, with the possible exception of the letter to the Romans, Paul's letters show little evidence that they were intended to endure as permanent documents. Paul, like other early Christians, expected an imminent Second Coming, and he wrote his letters to address immediate problems rather than to establish a lasting apparatus to perpetuate the church.

The four Gospels can be viewed as a history of the birth of faith. The Gospels all follow a similar pattern. They describe Jesus working miracles and preaching, but failing to convince many people of his divinity until his resurrection. The triumphant moment in the Gospels comes when the apostles witness the reborn Jesus and have their faith confirmed. The entire story of the Gospels is designed to stress the importance of faith for the Christian. Indeed, practically the only factor that separated these early Christians from the nonbelieving Jews was faith in Jesus. Nowhere in the Gospels, however, is the opposition between faith and law made so clear as in Romans. Paul elevates the role of faith, describing it as the sole means by which people can attain salvation. Through Jesus's self-sacrifice, Paul teaches, God gave men the free gift of a covenant of salvation. It is only by faith in Jesus that one attains salvation.

THE FIRST LETTER OF PAUL TO THE CORINTHIANS (1 CORINTHIANS)

INTRODUCTION

There is a general consensus among scholars that 1 Corinthians was written by the important early Christian missionary Paul of Tarsus. In late 56 or early 57 A.D., Paul was in the city of Ephesus in Asia Minor. From there, writing with his collaborator Sosthenes, he addressed a series of letters to the Greek city of Corinth, which he had visited between 50 and 52 A.D., and where he had converted both Jews and Gentiles to the Christian faith. Corinth was located on the isthmus connecting the Peloponnesian peninsula to the Greek mainland, and its advantageous location allowed it to become a prosperous merchant city. Prosperity, however, brought pagan hedonism. Corinth developed a reputation, widespread throughout the ancient world, for sexual license. Paul's letters to the Christians at Corinth address his concern over a pressing issue: the rampant immorality associated with the paganism of Corinth. This immorality had begun to infect the Corinthian church. Paul was deeply concerned for the spiritual health of the Corinthian church, which had been deprived of his guidance for several years. As a result, Paul corresponded at greater length with the Corinthian church than with any of the other communities that he established. The New Testament preserves two of these letters, 1 and 2 Corinthians, and makes reference to at least one other lost letter (1 Cor. 5:9).

SUMMARY

Paul begins 1 Corinthians with a greeting to "the church of God that is in Corinth," in which he offers thanks for the faith and strength of the Corinthian church (1:2). He immediately begins, however, to list and address the problems that plague that church. The first problem, to which he devotes almost four chapters, concerns factionalism within the church. Paul has heard that the Corinthian church has divided itself according to the various preachers of the Gospel: "each of you says, 'I belong to Paul,' or 'I belong to Apollos,' or 'I belong to Cephas,' or 'I belong to Christ'" (1:12). Paul stresses that each preacher of the Gospel is merely a servant of Jesus, and that all believers should be united in Jesus. The faithful should put aside their differences and remember that "[a]ll things are yours. . . . You belong to Christ, and Christ belongs to God" (3:23). The place of the preachers is not to establish themselves as leaders among men; instead, "[p]eople should think of us as servants of Christ" (4:1).

Paul enumerates various immoral tendencies of the Corinthian Christians. He cautions them to condemn sexual immorality within the church. Membership in the community of the faithful, he teaches, means that the church faithful must adjudicate moral matters amongst themselves, chastising and expelling sinners. In response to questions put to him about specific confusions over religious practice, Paul sets forth a principle that becomes embedded in church doctrine: "To the unmarried . . . I say: it is well for them to remain unmarried as I am. But if they are not practicing self-control, they should marry" (7:8–9). Paul advocates freedom of conscience within the bounds of faith. He does not mandate circumcision, although many early Christians, who were practically all Jewish, assumed that circumcision was a prerequisite for conversion to Christianity. Paul declares it permissible to eat food dedicated to false gods, provided that one does not compromise the conscience of another Christian by doing so.

In a break from his instruction, Paul spends Chapter 9 discussing his own case. He sees himself as a man who has sacrificed everything to preach the Gospel, forgoing material comfort and becoming all things to all people. Returning to his moral instruction, Paul invokes the example of the ancient Israelites, who were punished for their immorality and faithlessness, and exhorts the Corinthians to avoid idolatrous worship and sexual immorality. He explains to them that while it is not forbidden to eat certain foods, it is best to avoid offending people and to respect the consciences of others. Paul then speaks on public worship. He says that women must cover their heads during prayer, while men must pray with heads bared. When the Lord's Supper is commemorated, it must be celebrated in true communal fashion, and must be preceded by careful self-inspection.

In Chapters 12 and 14, Paul speaks of the regulation of spiritual gifts in the church of believers. There are many instances in the Corinthian church of people prophesying and speaking in tongues. These spiritual gifts are important because they help to strengthen the community. All gifts, and all believers, are indispensable to the church. Each believer is a part of the incarnated body of Jesus, and each fulfills his or her own particular function. But Paul prioritizes prophecy, with its clarity of message, over speaking in tongues, which is generally indecipherable and therefore cannot provide instruction to the community. Paul interrupts this discussion of spiritual gifts with Chapter 13, which has become known as the Hymn to Love, in which he expounds upon the importance of love: "And now faith, hope, and love abide, these three; and the greatest of these is love" (13:13).

Paul moves toward his conclusion with an exposition on the doctrinal question of the resurrection of the dead. He reminds the Corinthians of the core Christian doctrine. The resurrection of Jesus, he insists, is a cardinal point of the Christian faith. The future resurrection of all the dead stems from Jesus's own resurrection, and it is the future resurrection—the promise of eternal life—that makes Christian sacrifice meaningful: "If the dead are not raised, Let us eat and drink, for tomorrow we die" (15:33). Paul explains the nature of resurrection, noting that the physical body will not be resurrected. Rather, it is the spiritual body that is immortal. The immortality of the spiritual body signifies the true victory of faith over death, and Paul concludes, "Thanks be to God, who gives us the victory through our Lord Jesus Christ" (15:57). Finally, 1 Corinthians ends with Paul's instruction to the Corinthians to take up a collection for the benefit of the poor in Jerusalem. He expresses his hope that he will be able to visit Corinth soon, and in the meanwhile urges the Corinthians to accept his emissary Timothy with open arms. He charges them to "[k]eep alert, stand firm in your faith, be courageous, be strong. Let all that you do be done in love" (16:13–14).

ANALYSIS

In 1 Corinthians, through the issues that he chooses to address, Paul provides us with historical insight into the early Christian Church. It was a church without any single supreme authority. The missionaries and preachers who spread the Gospel in the decades after Jesus were by no means homogenous in their approaches to Christian doctrine and practice. Paul speaks of divisions in the church at Corinth that stem from perceived differences in the Gospel as preached by various missionaries. It seems that Paul, Apollos, and Cephas (the Aramaic name given to Peter) each had adherents in the Corinthian church. It is possible that the Christians at Corinth, recent converts who were inadequately instructed in Christianity, simply misunderstood the missionaries and believed doctrinal differences to exist. It is also possible that there were actual important differences between the Christianity of Peter and that of Paul. Instances of disagreements between early Christian leaders are both implicit and explicit in The New Testament. For instance, in Acts 15, it is evident that the apostles Peter and James are more conservative than Paul with regard to adhering to Jewish law. But it is also true that in Corinthians, Paul addresses a group of people with little knowledge of Paul's Jewish culture. A certain amount of confusion was probably inevitable.

Paul's letter is remarkable in that it exhorts the Corinthians toward unity rather than ideological division. He does not mandate resolving whatever differences may exist between the factions of the Corinthian church. Rather, he reminds them of the all-important unity that binds them and supersedes their differences. Throughout 1 Corinthians, the themes of unity and the importance of freedom of conscience within certain moral boundaries are constantly stressed. This freedom of conscience extends from doctrinal issues to questions of practice: for instance, Paul permits the Corinthians to eat food sacrificed to idols (10:26–27), in direct defiance of the principle established by the church leaders in Jerusalem (Acts 15:28–29). In his discussion of the various spiritual gifts granted to the faithful, Paul returns again to the theme of unity through diversity: "Now there are varieties of gifts, but the same Spirit; and there are varieties of services, but the same Lord" (12:4–5).

Paul's great commandment is to love. He hopes that love will bind the community together despite its differences, and lead people to achieve faith and godliness in anticipation of the imminent Second Coming. Paul attempts to unify the church by accepting varying beliefs and practices, but his emphasis on unity does not reflect any willingness to compromise his religious faith. Paul's accepting attitude has limitations, and 1 Corinthians is filled with Paul's righteous indignation. He does not hesitate to "say this to your shame" to the Corinthians, nor to chastise them for their moral misdeeds (15:34). In this letter, Paul assumes the voice of a stern but loving parent. He says, "In Christ Jesus I became your father" (4:15), and he tells the Corinthians, "I fed you with milk" (3:2). The family of believers is open to all who are faithful. Unlike many of the early Christians, Paul is willing to accept Gentile as well as Jew: "For in the one Spirit we were all baptized into one body . . . slaves or free" (12:13). But acceptance does not mean tolerance of repeated misdeeds and the refusal to repent: "Drive out the wicked person from among you" (5:13).

THE SECOND LETTER OF PAUL TO THE CORINTHIANS (2 CORINTHIANS)

INTRODUCTION

For in Christ Jesus you are all children of God through faith. As many of you as were baptized into Christ have clothed yourselves with Christ.

(See QUOTATIONS, *p. 67*)

The book known as 2 Corinthians is one of the fourteen New Testament letters that have traditionally been attributed to Paul, the great early Christian missionary preacher. While the authorship of many of these letters has been debated by modern scholars, there is a nearly unanimous consensus that 2 Corinthians was written by Paul. However, it was probably not written in the same form in which it appears today. Most scholars agree that 2 Corinthians is a combination of several letters written by Paul to the community of

Christian believers in the Greek city of Corinth. These letters would have been written at intervals of several months.

Following the sending of 1 Corinthians, Paul's disciple, Timothy, visited Corinth, and discovered that the situation there had not improved (Acts 19:21–22). Responding to this emergency, Paul paid an immediate visit to Corinth. He later refers to this visit as "painful" (2 Cor. 2:1). Apparently, an anonymous adversary publicly confronted Paul and undermined his authority. Whereas Paul had threatened to come to Corinth "with a stick" (1 Cor. 4:21), he was perceived on this later occasion as unimpressive and timid (2 Cor. 10:1). Leaving Corinth, Paul decided not to visit again until he had sent a letter "in much distress and anguish of the heart" (2 Cor. 2:4). It is possible that this letter has been lost. It is also possible that the letter was preserved and incorporated into the main body of 2 Corinthians as Chapters 10–13, an incongruous section whose shift in tone from the optimism of the preceding chapters is jarring, and which seems to rehash a controversy that has already been resolved. Soon after the Corinthians received this agonized letter, Titus, another disciple of Paul, visited Corinth, and found the community repentant as a result of Paul's letter (2 Cor. 7:5–13). Returning to Paul in Macedonia, Titus brought the happy news. In the early fall of 57 A.D., rejoicing at the news of the Corinthian repentance, Paul then wrote the letter to the church at Corinth that became 2 Corinthians.

SUMMARY

The letter that is 2 Corinthians begins with a long salutation and prayer of thanksgiving (1:1–11). Paul, writing with his disciple Timothy, thanks God for the encouragement he has received despite all the suffering he has recently undergone. The body of the letter begins with Paul's assertion that his behavior, especially toward the Corinthian church, has been inspired by the grace of God. His decision not to visit the Corinthians, and instead to write them a chastising letter "in much distress and anguish of the heart," is a decision made through God's grace (2:4). The agonized letter is intended not "to cause you pain, but to let you know the abundant love that I have for you" (2:4). He demonstrates this love by urging the repentant community to show love and forgiveness to the unnamed adversary who shamed Paul on the occasion of his previous, unsuccessful visit.

Paul spends much of the body of the letter justifying his own apostolic calling. As an envoy of God, spreading the Gospel of God, Paul is empowered to speak "with great boldness" (3:12). Paul takes pride in his ministry. His pride and fearlessness persist despite the many hardships to which he has been subjected as an apostle. Guided by faith, Paul does not hesitate to devote his life to the benefit of his human flock. However oppressed the ministers of God may be, Paul remembers that "we have a building from God," and that he will eventually be rewarded (5:1). Just as God will judge him justly, Paul asks the Corinthians to judge him justly: "We ourselves are well known to God, and I hope that we are also well known to your consciences" (5:11). Paul hopes to become "the righteousness of God," charged with the spreading of the Gospel, and he urges the Corinthians to be attentive to this Gospel (5:21). He concludes the section on the importance and authenticity of his calling with a brilliant evocation of the paradoxical status of the oppressed minister of God.

Paul's "heart is wide open" to the Corinthians, and he speaks honestly about his personal joy in his calling (6:11). He asks the Corinthians to reciprocally open their hearts, to treat him honestly, and to judge him fairly. After a brief interlude in which Paul pauses to warn the Corinthians against association with unbelievers, Paul continues with words of encouragement. Titus has told him of the Corinthian church's positive response to the agonized letter of chastisement that Paul sent them. Through the distress they felt at receiving his letter, they were led to repentance. Paul is now confident in the Corinthian church, and as a result he makes a request of them. In Chapters 8–9, he speaks of taking up a collection to support the church in Jerusalem, and urges the Corinthians to give generously: "As you excel in everything—in faith, in speech, in knowledge, in utmost eagerness, and in our love for you—so we want you to excel also in this generous undertaking" (8:7).

It has been suggested that Chapters 10–13 are the remnants of the agonized letter that Paul earlier sent to the Corinthians. Certainly, these chapters represent an abrupt shift from the triumphant tone of reconciliation in Chapters 7–9: Chapters 10–13 are a vehement defense of Paul's apostolic calling, and a strong repudiation of his critics. Paul speaks at length of the hardships he has undergone for the sake of his ministry: "I am a better one: with far greater labors, far more imprisonments, with countless floggings, and often near death" (11:23). Paul asserts that he is not inferior in importance even to the "super-apostles," the twelve original disciples appointed by Jesus. The favor of God is equally upon him, and he says that he has displayed "utmost patience, signs and wonders and mighty works" (12:12). Implicit is the idea that, since Paul is qualified as an apostle, the Corinthians should respect him and pay attention to his sermons. He is sending them this difficult letter, he tells them, "so that when I come, I may not have to be severe in using the authority that the Lord has given me for building up and not tearing down" (13:10). In conclusion, Paul wishes the Corinthians joy, communal harmony, and peace.

ANALYSIS

Modern scholars generally agree that at least seven New Testament letters can be attributed with reasonable certainty to Paul. Through his letters, and through his biography in Acts, Paul has become the most developed character in the New Testament. He exists for us not just as a towering religious figure, but as a deeply human personality. The letters give a startlingly clear picture of Paul— in his anger, despair, and triumph—throughout the many difficulties and victories he encounters during his ministry. Of all the New Testament books, 2 Corinthians is probably the most intensely personal. It is Paul's cry from the heart, a testimony to his devoted ministry to his communities of converts, but it is also revelatory of his human imperfections, his deep-seated insecurity and his quick temper.

Paul is a gifted correspondent. He has a talent for producing concise epigrams, such as "what can be seen is temporary, but what cannot be seen is eternal" (4:18). He is also a great poet. As he demonstrates in 2 Corinthians, he can be both gentle and severe at the same time. At one point, he says, "I am overjoyed in all our affliction" (7:4); later, he says, "If I come again, I will not be resilient" (13:2). He can also be self-effacingly humble and expansively boastful in the same breath, making comments such as, "I am not at all inferior to these super-apostles, even though I am nothing" (12:11).

In both 1 and 2 Corinthians, Paul spends a good deal of time rehearsing his qualifications for ministry and the extent of his martyrdom. Paul frequently seems insecure, perhaps as a result of the loose hierarchy of the early church. Paul may consider himself the equal of the "super-apostles," the twelve disciples appointed by Jesus himself as the heads of the church, but the fact remains that he is not one of the original apostles. Paul develops the term "super-apostle" to account for calling himself simply an "apostle," a title to which his claim was not well established. Paul believes that his epiphany on the road to Damascus in Acts 9 is as important a personal encounter with Jesus as any revelation experienced by the original Twelve Apostles. At one point, Paul's ministry is contrasted with that of Peter, the greatest of the original Twelve Apostles—a moment that could not have been comfortable for Paul (1 Cor. 1:12). Paul's dedication throughout the Corinthian correspondence to proving his equality with the "super-apostles" may well be a response to the implicit challenge to his apostolic station.

THE REVELATION TO JOHN (REVELATION)

INTRODUCTION

The Book of Revelation is strikingly different from the rest of the New Testament. It is populated by winged and wild creatures, locust plagues, and seven-headed beasts. Revelation is filled with obscure and fantastic symbolism, and it teems with mystical references. However, it lacks any real internal structure. Unlike the other New Testament books, which tend to mix narrative with sermon-style preaching, Revelation is essentially a long, uninterrupted record of a mystical vision, offering little interpretation for its intricate symbols. Revelation has been read for thousands of years as a code that, properly interpreted, can reveal the secrets of history and the end of the world. The numbers and symbols in Revelation have been read into any number of traumatic events in ancient and modern history.

Revelation was a product of this time of early growth and confusion, but also of a long Jewish tradition of apocalyptic literature. The Old Testament books of Ezekiel and Zechariah contain long apocalyptic segments. The most famous Old Testament apocalypse, the Book of Daniel, was written circa 165 B.C. The apocalyptic genre became more popular after 70 A.D., when the apocryphal apocalypses, 2 Baruch and 4 Ezra, were written in response to the destruction of the Jewish temple in Jerusalem by Roman armies. There is enough apocalyptic literature that it can be classified as a genre of its own, with its own particular characteristics. Some of these common features are revelations made to a human emissary through a supernatural agency, heavy symbolism, numerology with obscure significance, extravagant imagery, and concern about a cataclysmic day of judgment or the end of the world. Apocalyptic literature tends to take a deterministic view of history—that is,

SUMMARY & ANALYSIS

apocalypses are generally driven by the belief that history inexora-
bly follows a set path ordained by God. All of these characteristics
of the apocalyptic genre are present in Revelation.

SUMMARY

The introduction of Revelation names the author, John, and explains the immediacy of the message: the end of days is at hand.
John extends a greeting to the Christian communities in seven major
Near East cities in the name of the God of history. On the Sabbath,
John falls into a prophetic ecstasy. He sees a vision of a shining
Jesus, surrounded by seven stars and seven lamp-stands: these represent the seven churches of Asia. In 2:1–3:22, John is given orders
to deliver a message to each of the churches, addressing specific
strengths and failings of each church, providing encouragement to
some and driving others to repent before Judgment Day. Jesus reminds them that his coming is imminent. The first half of John's
revelatory experience begins with the opening of the heavenly door:
"Come up here," a voice calls to him, "I will show you what is to
take place in the future" (4:1). John sees God enthroned and surrounded by twenty-four elders.

Lightning flashes and thunder sounds. Old Testament angels
with six wings and many eyes sing praises to the Lord. God holds
a scroll sealed with seven seals, and nobody is worthy of breaking
the seals except Jesus, by virtue of his sacrifice. Jesus appears here
as "a Lamb standing as if it had been slaughtered," but also as "the
Lion of the tribe of Judah" (5:5–6). Breaking the first four seals,
Jesus releases the Four Horsemen of the Apocalypse: victory, war,
famine, and pestilence. When the fifth seal is broken, the souls of
martyrs cry out for justice, but they are urged to have patience until
the appointed number of people have been martyred. The breaking
of the sixth seal unleashes a massive cosmic upheaval that devas-
tates the world.

Before the breaking of the seventh seal, an angel marks 144,000
people—12,000 from each of the tribes of Israel—with the seal of
God to protect them from the coming devastation. Other righteous
people, too, are to be saved: a "great multitude . . . [of people] from
all the tribes and peoples and languages" have cleansed themselves
and they, too, will be protected (7:9). Finally, it is time to open the
seventh seal (8:1). But the opening of the seal is anticlimactic; when
it is opened, it is revealed that there are seven trumpets that need to
be blown. Four of the trumpets blow, each bringing with it disaster

and destruction, with fire falling from the sky (8:6–12). With the fifth trumpet, the chimney leading out of the Abyss is unlocked, and bizarre locusts emerge in the smoke, stinging anyone unmarked by God's seal. The sixth trumpet unleashes a vast troop of cavalry who kill "a third of humankind" (9:18). However, the survivors nevertheless refuse to stop worshipping idols and behaving immorally. An angel descends from heaven, announcing the imminent fulfillment of "the mystery of God" with the blowing of the seventh trumpet (10:7).

The prophet is ordered to consume a scroll, which will taste sweet but be bitter in his stomach (8:10). He is told that two prophets will arise to preach the word of God in Jerusalem, but will be killed after 1,260 days by "the beast that comes up from the bottomless pit" (11:7). God will revive these prophets, and will strike Jerusalem with a powerful earthquake. Finally, the seventh trumpet blows, and John hears voices shouting, "The kingdom of the world has become the kingdom of our Lord and of his Messiah, and he will reign forever and ever" (11:15). The moment for justice, punishment, and triumph has arrived, with lighting, thunder, earthquakes, and hail.

The second half of Revelation begins with the opening of God's sanctuary in heaven. A woman "clothed with the sun, with the moon under her feet," gives birth to a child who is almost eaten by a huge red dragon with seven heads and ten horns (12:1). The child is saved from the dragon and brought to heaven. The archangel Michael makes war on the dragon, who is Satan, defeats him, and drives him from heaven. The dragon continues to pursue the woman, who yet again escapes him. Instead, he makes war on her children. The dragon delegates his power to a fantastical creature identified only as "the beast," who makes war on the saints and curses God (13:4). A false prophet, "another beast," arises and convinces people to worship the first beast (13:11). The prophet sees Jesus and his 144,000 righteous followers entrenched on Mount Zion in Jerusalem. He hears the news that the Day of Judgment is at hand, and that Babylon the Great—probably symbolic of the Roman Empire—has fallen. Angels begin to spill out of the blood of the wicked like wine from a winepress. While the righteous sing hymns to Moses and Jesus, seven angels empty seven bowls of plagues across the Earth, bringing suffering and destruction to the wicked. People refuse to repent, and instead curse God. With the pouring out of the seventh bowl, "it is done" (16:17).

John is shown a vision of the Whore of Babylon, who symbolizes the Roman Empire. An angel announces the fall of Babylon and warns God's faithful to abandon Rome, lest they be punished together with the wicked. Those wicked people who made their livings from Rome's trade will mourn her downfall, but the righteous will rejoice. Many voices surrounding the throne of God sing his praises at the news, and announce that the Lamb, Jesus, is soon to be wedded to his "bride," the faithful of God (19:7). John is ordered to write the wedding announcement: "Blessed are those who are invited to the wedding supper of the Lamb" (19:9). In the final battle, the gates of heaven open, and Jesus, clad now as a warrior named "Faithful and True," leads the hosts of heaven in a war against the beast and the kings of the Earth (19:11). The beast and his false prophet are hurled into a fiery lake, and the other opponents of Jesus are killed. Together with the saints, Jesus reigns for 1,000 glorious years. At the end of the 1,000 years, Satan gathers his forces, Gog and Magog, and again leads them into battle against the saints, but they are consumed by fire. Satan, too, is hurled into the fiery pit. On the Day of Judgment, which follows immediately, everyone is resurrected and judged "according to their works" (20:12). After Judgment Day, John sees a vision of "a new heaven and a new earth," and a new holy city of Jerusalem descended from heaven (21:1). The New Jerusalem is a picture of shining perfection, carved of precious stones and lit by the glory of God and Jesus, who are present in Jerusalem instead of a temple. John is commanded to publicize the vision that he has received: "Do not seal up the words of the prophesy of this book, for the time is near" (22:10). In the conclusion of Revelation, Jesus himself promises that God will come soon to reward the righteous and punish the wicked.

ANALYSIS

The Book of Revelation was probably written sometime between 81 and 89 A.D. by a man named John, in and around the cities in Asia Minor. Some scholars contend that Revelation indeed talks about the future, but it primarily seeks to understand the present, a time that was almost certainly one of extreme stress for Christians. Revelation itself indicates that John understood that a persecution of Christians living in western Asia Minor was imminent, and that the persecution would come from the Romans, who would make demands for emperor worship that the Christians would have to resist. John's revelation is an attempt to persuade the small churches to turn away from imperial cult worship and toward the true God, who was in charge of history and who will triumph in the end. Revelation seeks to accommodate the contradiction of the triumph of God in history with the continued oppressive rule of the Romans.

Revelation's heavy use of imagination and provocative symbolism is central to its rhetorical power. Revelation turns to poetics and aesthetics to depict the imperial city of Rome as a beast, stating that "its feet were like a bear's and its mouth was like a lion's mouth" (13:2). The beast has ten horns and seven heads and carries on its back "Babylon the great, mother of whores, and of the earth's abominations" (17:5). Babylon, who is "drunk with the blood of the saints and the blood of the witnesses to Jesus," represents the Roman Empire (17:6). She is eventually judged by the more powerful God, who causes her fall in Revelation's climax: "He has judged the great whore who corrupted the earth with her fornication, and he has avenged on her the blood of his servants. . . . Fallen, fallen is Babylon the great!" (14:8, 19:2).

John's potent imagery is not only a "call for the endurance and faith of the saints" (13:10), but it also tries to move the audience to a decision to turn away from the beast "so that you do not take part in her sins" (18:4), and instead to turn toward the God of justice who "will wipe away every tear from their eyes" (21:4). Revelation persuades Christians to stake their lives on that decision. In Babylon, everything is for sale. John does not hedge about the immorality of such disparities between the rich and the poor. When Babylon is destroyed, neither God, Christ, the saints, the apostles, nor the prophets mourn. Those who are upset are "the merchants of the earth" (18:11) and "all whose trade is on the sea" (18:17). In addition, "the kings of the earth, who committed fornication and lived in luxury with her will weep and wail" (18:9).

IMPORTANT QUOTATIONS EXPLAINED

1. But to what will I compare this generation? It is like
    children sitting in the marketplaces and calling to one
    another, "We played the flute for you, and you did not
    dance; we wailed, and you did not mourn." For John
    came neither eating nor drinking, and they say, "He has a
    demon," the Son of Man came eating and drinking, and
    they say, "Look, a glutton and a drunkard, a friend of tax
    collectors and sinners!" Yet wisdom is vindicated by her
    deeds. (Matthew 11:16–19)

Throughout the New Testament, there are references to Jesus as the
wisdom of God, and here Matthew makes the association explicit.
Wisdom in Jewish tradition bears a variety of meanings, but the
most dominant role wisdom takes on is that of a teacher calling out
to the public to take him in (Prov. 1:20–21, 9:3). This concept of
wisdom correlates well with Matthew's overall definition of Christ's
nature, which focuses on Jesus's role as a teacher, instructor, and
sage (Matthew 11:1, 9:35).

In this parable, Jesus and John the Baptist can be interpreted
to be the figures who call out from the marketplace, play the flute,
dance, wail, and mourn. Those who will not join them are "this
generation," which will not hear God's message. This interpretation
is in keeping with the biblical figure of wisdom, which calls out to
the public from marketplaces, crossroads, portals, and streets (Prov.
1:20–21, 8:1–3) and is met with similar rejection (Prov. 8:36–38).
Wisdom says, "I have called and you refused, have stretched out my
hand and no one heeded" (Prov. 1:24–25). Wisdom opens the community and widens participation. Jesus/Wisdom is justified by the
deeds that recognize all Israelites as its children: "the blind receive
their sight, the lame walk, the lepers are cleansed, the deaf hear, the
dead are raised, and the poor have good news brought to them"
(Matthew 4–5). While these deeds justify Jesus, they are the source
of Jesus's rejection as a "glutton and a drunkard, friend of tax collectors and sinners" (Matthew 11:18).

2. In the beginning was the Word, and the Word was with
    God, and the Word was God. He was in the beginning
    with God. All things came into being through him, and
    without him not one thing came into being. What has
    come into being in him was life, and the life was the light
    of all people. The light that shines in the darkness, and the
    darkness did not overcome it. (John 1:1–5)

John's emphasis on Jesus as the Word of God incarnated is indebted
both to Greek philosophy and to his Jewish heritage. The Greeks
developed the concept of a divine force governing the balance
between binary opposites in the universe. They called this force
Logos, best translated as "Word" or "Reason." In many Greek
conceptions, it is Logos that determines the balance between light
and darkness, flesh and spirit. A world without Logos, the Greeks
believed, would be chaos. The influence of the concept of the Logos
was felt strongly by the Jewish sect knows as the Essenes, ascetics
who believed that the world was shaped by struggles between opposing forces. John takes his philosophical inspiration, which manifests
itself through his Christology and theology, from the Greeks via the
Essenes. Jesus is the Word, the Logos, who is the instrument of total
victory of light over darkness, its binary opposite: "What has come
into being in him was life. And the life was the light of all people"
(John 1:4). John's reference to the Essene and Greek systems of philosophy to explain Jesus's origin and significance is reflective of his
Gospel's careful pedagogical style. More than the authors of the
other Gospels, John is concerned with explaining significance rather
than recording facts.

3. For in Christ Jesus you are all children of God through
    faith. As many of you as were baptized into Christ have
    clothed yourselves with Christ. There is no longer Jew or
    Greek, there is no longer slave or free, there is no longer
    male or female; for all of you are one in Christ Jesus.
    (Galatians 3:26–28)

The meaning of this passage, written by Paul in a letter to the church
at Galatians, is still very much at the center of controversy among
biblical scholars today. Some scholars contend that Paul's notion of
equality here speaks of a spiritual or transcendental equality rather
than a social equality. This interpretation diminishes the social implications of the texts. Others claim that Paul has in mind social or
ecclesiastical equality with serious political implications. Biblical
scholar Elisabeth Schüssler Fiorenza argues that among Christ's followers, status differences are no longer valid. Statements such as
Paul's reflect an equality that many scholars claim was present in the
vision and practice of the earliest Christian missionary movement.
Currently, many feminist and other biblical scholars are recon-
structing the early Christian community to find important traces of
social egalitarianism. Many point to this passage as one of the most
important indicators of the egalitarian ideals of the early Christian
community.

QUOTATIONS

4.   A sower went out to sow his seed; and as he sowed, some fell on the path, and was trampled on, and the birds of the air ate it up. Some fell on the rock; and as it grew up, it withered for lack of moisture. Some fell among the thorns, and the thorns grew with it and choked it. Some fell into good soil and grew, and when it grew it produced a hundredfold. (Luke 8:5–8)

The parable of the sower is found in Matthew, Mark, and even some writings that are not in the Christian canon, such as the Gospel of Thomas. Because the parable is found in a relatively uniform manner in various places, and because scholars have concluded that Jesus spoke in parables, we can assume that this parable did in fact come from the historical figure of Jesus. The parable stresses the mystery of the unexpected acceptance of the Kingdom of God despite much failure in hearing, being heard, and understanding. In Mark's version of the parable (Mark 4:14–20), Jesus interprets the parable for his inner circle of followers, though most scholars conclude that such interpretations were later additions by the early church. Mark's allegorical interpretation reads the sower as the speaker of the good news, and the seed as the word with potential to take root and "bear fruit" (4:20). The path is interpreted as hearers who are vulnerable to various symbolic dangers. Birds represent the evil that takes away the work sowed in Christ's followers. Rocky ground represents hearers who eagerly accept the word with enthusiasm but eventually fall away. Thorns represent listeners who are consumed with secular matters. The good soil represents hearers who patiently accept the word and eventually bear fruit.

5.   Now before the festival of the Passover, Jesus knew that his hour had come to depart from this world and go to the Father. Having loved his own who were in the world, he loved them to the end. [He] got up from the table, took off his outer robe, and tied a towel around himself. Then he poured water into a basin and began to wash the disciples' feet. . . . After he had washed their feet, had put on his robe, and had returned to the table, he said to them, ". . . I have set you an example, that you also should do as I have done to you. Very truly I tell you, servants are not greater than their master, nor are messengers greater than the one who sent them. If you know these things, you are blessed if you do them." (John 13:1, 4–5, 12–17)

Here, Jesus forms and participates in a community based on service and love to one another, setting an example to be followed by each of his disciples. For John's community, the purpose of the foot-cleansing here is not a ritual cleansing, such as Peter thinks, but the completion of Jesus's full revelation of service and love. Throughout John's Gospel, as this passage indicates, the exercise of leadership and power in the new ministry of Jesus is not one of ecclesiastical hierarchy, but one of love and service among a community of friends.

KEY FACTS

AUTHOR

MATTHEW: Circulated anonymously until the second century A.D., when it was attributed to Matthew

MARK: John Mark, a close interpreter of Peter

LUKE, ACTS: An anonymous Gentile Christian

JOHN: Unknown

ROMANS, 1 AND 2 CORINTHIANS: Paul of Tarsus

REVELATION: A man named John from the island of Patmos

TYPE OF WORK

MATTHEW, MARK, LUKE, JOHN, ACTS: Gospel, historical narrative

ROMANS, 1 AND 2 CORINTHIANS: Epistle, letter

REVELATION: Written record of a vision

LANGUAGE

Greek

TIME AND PLACE WRITTEN

MATTHEW: 85–90 A.D. in Antioch of Syria

MARK: Around 70 A.D. in Syria or Rome

LUKE, ACTS: 80–125 A.D.

ROMANS: 55–56 A.D.

1 AND 2 CORINTHIANS: 53–54 A.D. in Ephesus

REVELATION: 81–96 A.D. in Asia Minor

MAJOR CONFLICT

MATTHEW: Israel's rejection of Jesus

MARK, LUKE, ACTS: The public doubt of Jesus's role as the Son of God

ROMANS: The difficulty of incorporating both Jews and Gentiles into the early church

1 AND 2 CORINTHIANS: The disunity caused by Corinth's extreme religious piety

THEMES

The New Testament's relation to the Old Testament; salvation for social outcasts; salvation through faith in Christ

MOTIF

Geography

SYMBOLS

The kingdom of heaven; the Good Samaritan; water, bread, and light; the olive tree; the body

STUDY QUESTIONS

1. *What are the significant differences between Matthew's and Luke's narratives of Jesus's infancy?*

The different purposes with which Matthew and Luke approach their narratives influence the ways that they tell the story of Christ's birth. Because both authors are primarily interested in establishing the divinity of Christ, they both call Jesus's birth miraculous, and cite God alone as the creator of Jesus's life. But Matthew, who is interested in the Jewish lineage of Christ and the relationship between Christ's teachings and the Judaic tradition, focuses on the social ramifications of Mary's pregnancy more than Luke does. Matthew lauds Joseph for not abandoning his fiancée, even though Jewish custom dictates that pregnancy outside of wedlock is so shameful as to require a man to abandon his future wife. Luke's narrative seeks to declare the good news of Christ's birth to the poor and outcast, including women. As a result, Luke focuses on the humility of Jesus's origins, pointing out that Jesus's birth occurs in humble peasant surroundings. Luke also exalts Mary for her courage, making her a prominent female character with whom women in his audience might be able to sympathize.

2. *How does the historical context of the Book of*
    Revelation affect its content?

The Book of Revelation was written between 81 and 96 A.D. by a
leader in a small church community on the island of Patmos. This
community experienced persecution by the Roman Empire, which
forced early Christians to put their allegiance to the empire before
their allegiance to religion. When the Book of Revelation was written, the Roman Empire was expanding, and many Christians re-
sisted both this expansion and Roman cults. Much of the Book of
Revelation focuses on the contrast between the evils of the Roman
Empire, personified as the two beasts in Revelation 13, and the true
Christian God, who, according to Revelation, will "wipe away every tear" (21:4). Furthermore, in the first century A.D., apocalyptic literature like the Book of Revelation was very common, and
Revelation contains many of the conventions of this literary form.
Apocalyptic literature involves revelations that claim to predict
future events, whereas previous revelations had only claimed to
deliver the word of God. Moreover, apocalyptic literature almost
always follows dual narratives of hope and despair, at once describing the current evils of the world and promising a figure who would
save the righteous or faithful from the ultimate demise of the sinful
world. The Book of Revelation uses the conventions of a popular
literary form to address a pressing contemporary event. By describing equally vivid scenes of destruction and salvation, the Book of
Revelation attempts to instill a hatred for the Roman Empire and
strengthen faith in Christianity.

3. *What is Paul's relationship to Judaism, and what does he see as the relationship between Judaism and Christianity?*

Paul of Tarsus calls himself a "Jew of Jews," and never would have thought of himself otherwise. Like most of the early followers of Jesus, he came from a Jewish background, and saw Jesus's teachings as an extension rather than a challenge to Judaism. However, the two religions come into conflict on many points. For Paul, the most significant conflict is between the Jewish idea that people will be judged according to their good or bad deeds on Earth and the Christian idea that faith in Christ is the only way to earn eternal salvation. Paul's egalitarian approach emphasizes equality rather than inequality between Jews and Gentiles, saying that only with faith in God and Jesus Christ is salvation possible. His writing does not reconcile this conflict, but he does express his belief that the people of Israel are chosen and merit special grace, but that the death and resurrection of Jesus Christ could also assure a promise of grace. Paul's belief that forgiveness and love are given to all people, Jew and Gentile alike, made him a popular missionary. Rather than preaching religion as an exclusionary institution, his writing suggests that there is room within Christianity for people of different backgrounds. He views his belief as a renewed form of Judaism, not as an abandonment of his tradition.

How to Write Literary Analysis

The Literary Essay: A Step-by-Step Guide

When you read for pleasure, your only goal is enjoyment. You might find yourself reading to get caught up in an exciting story, to learn about an interesting time or place, or just to pass time. Maybe you're looking for inspiration, guidance, or a reflection of your own life. There are as many different, valid ways of reading a book as there are books in the world.

When you read a work of literature in an English class, however, you're being asked to read in a special way: you're being asked to perform *literary analysis*. To analyze something means to break it down into smaller parts and then examine how those parts work, both individually and together. Literary analysis involves examining all the parts of a novel, play, short story, or poem—elements such as character, setting, tone, and imagery—and thinking about how the author uses those elements to create certain effects.

A literary essay isn't a book review: you're not being asked whether or not you liked a book or whether you'd recommend it to another reader. A literary essay also isn't like the kind of book report you wrote when you were younger, where your teacher wanted you to summarize the book's action. A high school- or college-level literary essay asks, "How does this piece of literature actually work?" "How does it do what it does?" and, "Why might the author have made the choices he or she did?"

The Seven Steps

No one is born knowing how to analyze literature; it's a skill you learn and a process you can master. As you gain more practice with this kind of thinking and writing, you'll be able to craft a method that works best for you. But until then, here are seven basic steps to writing a well-constructed literary essay:

1. *Ask questions*
2. *Collect evidence*
3. *Construct a thesis*

4. *Develop and organize arguments*
5. *Write the introduction*
6. *Write the body paragraphs*
7. *Write the conclusion*

---

1. ASK QUESTIONS

When you're assigned a literary essay in class, your teacher will often provide you with a list of writing prompts. Lucky you! Now all you have to do is choose one. Do yourself a favor and pick a topic that interests you. You'll have a much better (not to mention easier) time if you start off with something you enjoy thinking about. If you are asked to come up with a topic by yourself, though, you might start to feel a little panicked. Maybe you have too many ideas—or none at all. Don't worry. Take a deep breath and start by asking yourself these questions:

- **What struck you?** Did a particular image, line, or scene linger in your mind for a long time? If it fascinated you, chances are you can draw on it to write a fascinating essay.

- **What confused you?** Maybe you were surprised to see a character act in a certain way, or maybe you didn't understand why the book ended the way it did. Confusing moments in a work of literature are like a loose thread in a sweater: if you pull on it, you can unravel the entire thing. Ask yourself why the author chose to write about that character or scene the way he or she did and you might tap into some important insights about the work as a whole.

- **Did you notice any patterns?** Is there a phrase that the main character uses constantly or an image that repeats throughout the book? If you can figure out how that pattern weaves through the work and what the significance of that pattern is, you've almost got your entire essay mapped out.

- **Did you notice any contradictions or ironies?** Great works of literature are complex; great literary essays recognize and explain those complexities. Maybe the title (*Happy Days*) totally disagrees with the book's subject matter (hungry orphans dying in the woods). Maybe the main character acts one way around his family and a completely different way around his friends and associates. If you can find a way to explain a work's contradictory elements, you've got the seeds of a great essay.

At this point, you don't need to know exactly what you're going to say about your topic; you just need a place to begin your exploration. You can help direct your reading and brainstorming by formulating your topic as a *question,* which you'll then try to answer in your essay. The best questions invite critical debates and discussions, not just a rehashing of the summary. Remember, you're looking for something you can *prove or argue* based on evidence you find in the text. Finally, remember to keep the scope of your question in mind: is this a topic you can adequately address within the word or page limit you've been given? Conversely, is this a topic big enough to fill the required length?

GOOD QUESTIONS

> *"Are Romeo and Juliet's parents responsible for the deaths of their children?"*
> *"Why do pigs keep showing up in* LORD OF THE FLIES?"
> *"Are Dr. Frankenstein and his monster alike? How?"*

BAD QUESTIONS

> *"What happens to Scout in* TO KILL A MOCKINGBIRD?"
> *"What do the other characters in* JULIUS CAESAR *think about Caesar?"*
> *"How does Hester Prynne in* THE SCARLET LETTER *remind me of my sister?"*

---

2. COLLECT EVIDENCE

Once you know what question you want to answer, it's time to scour the book for things that will help you answer the question. Don't worry if you don't know what you want to say yet—right now you're just collecting ideas and material and letting it all percolate. Keep track of passages, symbols, images, or scenes that deal with your topic. Eventually, you'll start making connections between these examples and your thesis will emerge.

Here's a brief summary of the various parts that compose each and every work of literature. These are the elements that you will analyze in your essay, and which you will offer as evidence to support your arguments. For more on the parts of literary works, see the Glossary of Literary Terms at the end of this section.

ELEMENTS OF STORY These are the *what*s of the work—what happens, where it happens, and to whom it happens.

- **Plot:** All of the events and actions of the work.

- **Character:** The people who act and are acted upon in a literary work. The main character of a work is known as the *protagonist*.

- **Conflict:** The central tension in the work. In most cases, the protagonist wants something, while opposing forces (antagonists) hinder the protagonist's progress.

- **Setting:** When and where the work takes place. Elements of setting include location, time period, time of day, weather, social atmosphere, and economic conditions.

- **Narrator:** The person telling the story. The narrator may straightforwardly report what happens, convey the subjective opinions and perceptions of one or more characters, or provide commentary and opinion in his or her own voice.

- **Themes:** The main idea or message of the work—usually an abstract idea about people, society, or life in general. A work may have many themes, which may be in tension with one another.

ELEMENTS OF STYLE These are the *how*s—how the characters speak, how the story is constructed, and how language is used throughout the work.

- **Structure and organization:** How the parts of the work are assembled. Some novels are narrated in a linear, chronological fashion, while others skip around in time. Some plays follow a traditional three- or five-act structure, while others are a series of loosely connected scenes. Some authors deliberately leave gaps in their works, leaving readers to puzzle out the missing information. A work's structure and organization can tell you a lot about the kind of message it wants to convey.

- **Point of view:** The perspective from which a story is told. In *first-person point of view*, the narrator involves him or herself in the story. ("I went to the store"; "We watched in horror as the bird slammed into the window.") A first-person narrator is usually the protagonist of the work, but not always. In *third-person point of view*, the narrator does not participate in the story. A third-person narrator may closely follow a specific character, recounting that individual character's thoughts or experiences, or it may be what we call an *omniscient* narrator. Omniscient narrators see and know all: they can witness any event in any time or place and are privy to the inner thoughts and feelings of all characters. Remember that the narrator and the author are not the same thing!

- **Diction:** Word choice. Whether a character uses dry, clinical language or flowery prose with lots of exclamation points can tell you a lot about his or her attitude and personality.

- **Syntax:** Word order and sentence construction. Syntax is a crucial part of establishing an author's narrative voice. Ernest Hemingway, for example, is known for writing in very short, straightforward sentences, while James Joyce characteristically wrote in long, incredibly complicated lines.

- **Tone:** The mood or feeling of the text. Diction and syntax often contribute to the tone of a work. A novel written in short, clipped sentences that use small, simple words might feel brusque, cold, or matter-of-fact.

- **Imagery:** Language that appeals to the senses, representing things that can be seen, smelled, heard, tasted, or touched.

- **Figurative language:** Language that is not meant to be interpreted literally. The most common types of figurative language are *metaphors* and *similes,* which compare two unlike things in order to suggest a similarity between them—for example, "All the world's a stage," or "The moon is like a ball of green cheese." (Metaphors say one thing *is* another thing; similes claim that one thing is *like* another thing.)

---

3. Construct a Thesis

When you've examined all the evidence you've collected and know how you want to answer the question, it's time to write your thesis statement. A *thesis* is a claim about a work of literature that needs to be supported by evidence and arguments. The thesis statement is the heart of the literary essay, and the bulk of your paper will be spent trying to prove this claim. A good thesis will be:

- **Arguable.** "*The Great Gatsby* describes New York society in the 1920s" isn't a thesis—it's a fact.

- **Provable through textual evidence.** "*Hamlet* is a confusing but ultimately very well-written play" is a weak thesis because it offers the writer's personal opinion about the book. Yes, it's arguable, but it's not a claim that can be proved or supported with examples taken from the play itself.

- **Surprising.** "Both George and Lenny change a great deal in *Of Mice and Men*" is a weak thesis because it's obvious. A really strong thesis will argue for a reading of the text that is not immediately apparent.

- **Specific.** "Dr. Frankenstein's monster tells us a lot about the human condition" is *almost* a really great thesis statement, but it's still too vague. What does the writer mean by "a lot"? *How* does the monster tell us so much about the human condition?

Good Thesis Statements

Question: In *Romeo and Juliet*, which is more powerful in shaping the lovers' story: fate or foolishness?

Thesis: "Though Shakespeare defines Romeo and Juliet as 'star-crossed lovers' and images of stars and planets appear throughout the play, a closer examination of that celestial imagery reveals that the stars are merely witnesses to the characters' foolish activities and not the causes themselves."

Question: How does the bell jar function as a symbol in Sylvia Plath's *The Bell Jar*?

Thesis: "A bell jar is a bell-shaped glass that has three basic uses: to hold a specimen for observation, to contain gases, and to maintain a vacuum. The bell jar appears in each of these capacities in *The Bell Jar,* Plath's semi-autobiographical novel, and each appearance marks a different stage in Esther's mental breakdown."

Question: Would Piggy in *The Lord of the Flies* make a good island leader if he were given the chance?

Thesis: "Though the intelligent, rational, and innovative Piggy has the mental characteristics of a good leader, he ultimately lacks the social skills necessary to be an effective one. Golding emphasizes this point by giving Piggy a foil in the charismatic Jack, whose magnetic personality allows him to capture and wield power effectively, if not always wisely."

4. DEVELOP AND ORGANIZE ARGUMENTS

The reasons and examples that support your thesis will form the middle paragraphs of your essay. Since you can't really write your thesis statement until you know how you'll structure your argument, you'll probably end up working on steps 3 and 4 at the same time.

There's no single method of argumentation that will work in every context. One essay prompt might ask you to compare and contrast two characters, while another asks you to trace an image through a given work of literature. These questions require different kinds of answers and therefore different kinds of arguments. Below, we'll discuss three common kinds of essay prompts and some strategies for constructing a solid, well-argued case.

TYPES OF LITERARY ESSAYS

- **Compare and contrast**

  Compare and contrast the characters of Huck and Jim in THE ADVENTURES OF HUCKLEBERRY FINN.

  Chances are you've written this kind of essay before. In an academic literary context, you'll organize your arguments the same way you would in any other class. You can either go *subject by subject* or *point by point*. In the former, you'll discuss one character first and then the second. In the latter, you'll choose several traits (attitude toward life, social status, images and metaphors associated with the character) and devote a paragraph to each. You may want to use a mix of these two approaches—for example, you may want to spend a paragraph a piece broadly sketching Huck's and Jim's personalities before transitioning into a paragraph or two that describes a few key points of comparison. This can be a highly effective strategy if you want to make a counterintuitive argument—that, despite seeming to be totally different, the two objects being compared are actually similar in a very important way (or vice versa). Remember that your essay should reveal something fresh or unexpected about the text, so think beyond the obvious parallels and differences.

- **Trace**

  Choose an image—for example, birds, knives, or eyes—and trace that image throughout MACBETH.

  Sounds pretty easy, right? All you need to do is read the play, underline every appearance of a knife in *Macbeth*, and then list them in your essay in the order they appear, right? Well, not exactly. Your teacher doesn't want a simple catalog of examples. He or she wants to see you make *connections* between those examples—that's the difference between summarizing and analyzing. In the *Macbeth* example above, think about the different contexts in which knives appear in the play and to what effect. In *Macbeth*, there are real knives and imagined knives; knives that kill and knives that simply threaten. Categorize and classify your examples to give them some order. Finally, always keep the overall effect in mind. After you choose and analyze your examples, you should come to some greater understanding about the work, as well as your chosen image, symbol, or phrase's role in developing the major themes and stylistic strategies of that work.

- **Debate**

    Is the society depicted in 1984 good for its citizens?

In this kind of essay, you're being asked to debate a moral, ethical, or aesthetic issue regarding the work. You might be asked to judge a character or group of characters (*Is Caesar responsible for his own demise?*) or the work itself (*Is JANE EYRE a feminist novel?*). For this kind of essay, there are two important points to keep in mind. First, don't simply base your arguments on your personal feelings and reactions. Every literary essay expects you to read and analyze the work, so search for evidence in the text. What do characters in *1984* have to say about the government of Oceania? What images does Orwell use that might give you a hint about his attitude toward the government? As in any debate, you also need to make sure that you define all the necessary terms before you begin to argue your case. What does it mean to be a "good" society? What makes a novel "feminist"? You should define your terms right up front, in the first paragraph after your introduction.

Second, remember that strong literary essays make contrary and surprising arguments. Try to think outside the box. In the *1984* example above, it seems like the obvious answer would be no, the totalitarian society depicted in Orwell's novel is *not* good for its citizens. But can you think of any arguments for the opposite side? Even if your final assertion is that the novel depicts a cruel, repressive, and therefore harmful society, acknowledging and responding to the counterargument will strengthen your overall case.

5. WRITE THE INTRODUCTION

Your introduction sets up the entire essay. It's where you present your topic and articulate the particular issues and questions you'll be addressing. It's also where you, as the writer, introduce yourself to your readers. A persuasive literary essay immediately establishes its writer as a knowledgeable, authoritative figure.

An introduction can vary in length depending on the overall length of the essay, but in a traditional five-paragraph essay it should be no longer than one paragraph. However long it is, your introduction needs to:

- **Provide any necessary context.** Your introduction should situate the reader and let him or her know what to expect. What book are you discussing? Which characters? What topic will you be addressing?

- **Answer the "So what?" question.** Why is this topic important, and why is your particular position on the topic noteworthy? Ideally, your introduction should pique the reader's interest by suggesting how your argument is surprising or otherwise counterintuitive. Literary essays make unexpected connections and reveal less-than-obvious truths.

- **Present your thesis.** This usually happens at or very near the end of your introduction.

- **Indicate the shape of the essay to come.** Your reader should finish reading your introduction with a good sense of the scope of your essay as well as the path you'll take toward proving your thesis. You don't need to spell out every step, but you do need to suggest the organizational pattern you'll be using.

Your introduction should not:

- **Be vague.** Beware of the two killer words in literary analysis: *interesting* and *important*. Of course the work, question, or example is interesting and important—that's why you're writing about it!

- **Open with any grandiose assertions.** Many student readers think that beginning their essays with a flamboyant statement such as, "Since the dawn of time, writers have been fascinated with the topic of free will," makes them sound important and commanding. You know what? It actually sounds pretty amateurish.

- **Wildly praise the work.** Another typical mistake student writers make is extolling the work or author. Your teacher doesn't need to be told that "Shakespeare is perhaps the greatest writer in the English language." You can mention a work's reputation in passing—by referring to *The Adventures of Huckleberry Finn* as "Mark Twain's enduring classic," for example—but don't make a point of bringing it up unless that reputation is key to your argument.

- **Go off-topic.** Keep your introduction streamlined and to the point. Don't feel the need to throw in all kinds of bells and whistles in order to impress your reader—just get to the point as quickly as you can, without skimping on any of the required steps.

6. WRITE THE BODY PARAGRAPHS

Once you've written your introduction, you'll take the arguments you developed in step 4 and turn them into your body paragraphs. The organization of this middle section of your essay will largely be determined by the argumentative strategy you use, but no matter how you arrange your thoughts, your body paragraphs need to do the following:

- **Begin with a strong topic sentence.** Topic sentences are like signs on a highway: they tell the reader where they are and where they're going. A good topic sentence not only alerts readers to what issue will be discussed in the following paragraph but also gives them a sense of what argument will be made *about* that issue. "Rumor and gossip play an important role in *The Crucible*" isn't a strong topic sentence because it doesn't tell us very much. "The community's constant gossiping creates an environment that allows false accusations to flourish" is a much stronger topic sentence— it not only tells us *what* the paragraph will discuss (gossip) but *how* the paragraph will discuss the topic (by showing how gossip creates a set of conditions that leads to the play's climactic action).

- **Fully and completely develop a single thought.** Don't skip around in your paragraph or try to stuff in too much material. Body paragraphs are like bricks: each individual

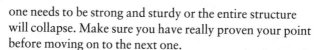

one needs to be strong and sturdy or the entire structure will collapse. Make sure you have really proven your point before moving on to the next one.

- **Use transitions effectively.** Good literary essay writers know that each paragraph must be clearly and strongly linked to the material around it. Think of each paragraph as a response to the one that precedes it. Use transition words and phrases such as *however, similarly, on the contrary, therefore,* and *furthermore* to indicate what kind of response you're making.

7. WRITE THE CONCLUSION

Just as you used the introduction to ground your readers in the topic before providing your thesis, you'll use the conclusion to quickly summarize the specifics learned thus far and then hint at the broader implications of your topic. A good conclusion will:

- **Do more than simply restate the thesis.** If your thesis argued that *The Catcher in the Rye* can be read as a Christian allegory, don't simply end your essay by saying, "And that is why *The Catcher in the Rye* can be read as a Christian allegory." If you've constructed your arguments well, this kind of statement will just be redundant.

- **Synthesize the arguments, not summarize them.** Similarly, don't repeat the details of your body paragraphs in your conclusion. The reader has already read your essay, and chances are it's not so long that they've forgotten all your points by now.

- **Revisit the "So what?" question.** In your introduction, you made a case for why your topic and position are important. You should close your essay with the same sort of gesture. What do your readers know now that they didn't know before? How will that knowledge help them better appreciate or understand the work overall?

- **Move from the specific to the general.** Your essay has most likely treated a very specific element of the work—a single character, a small set of images, or a particular passage. In your conclusion, try to show how this narrow discussion has wider implications for the work overall. If your essay on *To Kill a Mockingbird* focused on the character of Boo Radley, for example, you might want to include a bit in your conclusion about how he fits into the novel's larger message about childhood, innocence, or family life.

- **Stay relevant.** Your conclusion should suggest new directions of thought, but it shouldn't be treated as an opportunity to pad your essay with all the extra, interesting ideas you came up with during your brainstorming sessions but couldn't fit into the essay proper. Don't attempt to stuff in unrelated queries or too many abstract thoughts.

- **Avoid making overblown closing statements.** A conclusion should open up your highly specific, focused discussion, but it should do so without drawing a sweeping lesson about life or human nature. Making such observations may be part of the point of reading, but it's almost always a mistake in essays, where these observations tend to sound overly dramatic or simply silly.

A+ Essay Checklist

Congratulations! If you've followed all the steps we've outlined above, you should have a solid literary essay to show for all your efforts. What if you've got your sights set on an A+? To write the kind of superlative essay that will be rewarded with a perfect grade, keep the following rubric in mind. These are the qualities that teachers expect to see in a truly A+ essay. How does yours stack up?

- ✓ Demonstrates a thorough understanding of the book
- ✓ Presents an original, compelling argument
- ✓ Thoughtfully analyzes the text's formal elements
- ✓ Uses appropriate and insightful examples
- ✓ Structures ideas in a logical and progressive order
- ✓ Demonstrates a mastery of sentence construction, transitions, grammar, spelling, and word choice

Suggested Essay Topics

1. *Choose one New Testament parable that is found in more than one Gospel. Provide an analysis of the similarities and the differences between the versions. What is the significance of this comparison for understanding the distinctive theological perspectives of the Gospels?*

2. *Describe the similarities and differences among two of the Passion narratives (i.e., the trial and crucifixion). What is significant for the authors of these accounts? What is at stake in answering the question of who killed Jesus?*

3. *Consider the Book of Revelation. How might one be able to use the book in a contemporary learning context, without using it to claim salvation for the few and destruction for the many? Does it have anything to say to contemporary society?*

4. *The New Testament contains numerous discussions pertaining to the resurrection of Jesus. Compare and contrast a resurrection account in one of the Gospels to Paul's understanding of the living Christ in one of his letters.*

A+ Student Essay

Does the Gospel of Matthew present Jesus as a specifically Jewish messiah or as a universal savior?

Matthew, a Jewish author writing for a Jewish audience, is keenly interested in representing Jesus as the promised messiah of the Jews. At the same time, however, Matthew's Gospel was written sometime in the last two decades of the first century A.D., when the Jesus movement was spreading faster among Gentiles than among Jews. Therefore, as Matthew depicts Jesus as messiah to the Jews, he must also be careful not to alienate the growing population of Gentile followers. He accomplishes this by depicting Jesus as initially concerned only with Jews, and developing an interest in Gentiles only after it becomes clear that mainstream Jews do not view him as their messiah.

In his Gospel, Matthew links Jesus to Jewish tradition in multiple ways. When he reconstructs Jesus's genealogy, he explicitly traces Jesus's lineage all the way back to Abraham, the founding patriarch of Judaism. Additionally, Matthew alters Jesus's genealogy (in comparison to Luke) so that he can group Jesus's ancestors into sets of fourteen, a point to which he explicitly calls our attention. While the Gospel of Matthew was originally written in Greek, its Jewish audience would have been familiar with Hebrew, and in Hebrew the number fourteen is also the proper name *David*. Thus Matthew makes it clear that Jesus is both a direct descendant of Abraham and a new David, a messianic figure who has arrived to return the Jews to the glory of the Davidic Monarchy.

Matthew goes on to connect Jesus with another great Jewish figure, Moses. In contrast to Luke, Matthew claims that the infant Jesus was taken to Egypt to protect him from Herod. This allows Matthew to depict Jesus as coming up out of Egypt to lead his people, just as Moses did. Similarly, Matthew has Jesus perform ten healing miracles to parallel Moses' ten miracles (the plagues) in Egypt, and Matthew depicts Jesus wandering in the wilderness for forty days, an allusion to the way that the Book of Exodus shows Moses wandering in the wilderness for forty years. Matthew also shows Jesus to be the new Moses in the way that he is depicted as a lawgiver. Whereas Luke writes of Jesus delivering the beatitudes on a plain (the Sermon on the Plain), Matthew represents Jesus as climbing a mountain to receive laws from the deity and deliver them to the people (the Sermon on the Mount). This depiction is an echo of the way that Moses climbed the deity's sacred mountain to receive the commandments in the Book of Exodus. With all of these connections, Matthew leaves little doubt that he wants his readers to see Jesus as another link in the chain of great Jewish leaders.

Jesus's status as the Jewish messiah is underscored by the fact that Jesus explicitly states that he has come only to help "the lost sheep of the house of Israel." Jesus's mission to the Jews is derailed, however, by the way that mainstream Jews, the Pharisees in particular, reject his teachings. Jesus has several confrontations with the Pharisees, who never bend in their opposition to him. These tensions are heightened by the fact that Jesus not only attacks some of the Pharisees' practices but also goes so far as to alter the commandments given to Moses, claiming, for instance, that the prohibition on adultery extends to lustful thoughts, and that the prohibition on murder extends to feelings of anger. In making these changes to the sacred laws, Jesus offers a much stricter and more demanding form of faith than the Pharisees were prepared to accept.

Matthew solves the problem of how Jesus can be both the Jewish messiah and a universal savior by having Jesus use his rejection at the hands of the Pharisees as a basis for broadening his mission. After a particularly strident dispute with the Pharisees, Jesus has an encounter with a Gentile Canaanite woman. The woman asks Jesus to help her daughter, but Jesus initially refuses, saying that he was sent only to Jews and comparing Gentiles with dogs. The woman persists, however, and Jesus sees that her faith in him is great (and much greater than that of the Pharisees), so he changes his mind and heals her daughter. This switch from an exclusively Jewish mission to a more universal one foreshadows the final movement of the Gospel. In its closing moments, Matthew's Gospel shows Jesus returning from the dead to tell his followers to "make disciples of all nations." Jesus's transformation into a universal savior is complete.

GLOSSARY OF LITERARY TERMS

ANTAGONIST
> The entity that acts to frustrate the goals of the *protagonist*. The antagonist is usually another *character* but may also be a non-human force.

ANTIHERO / ANTIHEROINE
> A *protagonist* who is not admirable or who challenges notions of what should be considered admirable.

CHARACTER
> A person, animal, or any other thing with a personality that appears in a *narrative*.

CLIMAX
> The moment of greatest intensity in a text or the major turning point in the *plot*.

CONFLICT
> The central struggle that moves the *plot* forward. The conflict can be the *protagonist*'s struggle against fate, nature, society, or another person.

FIRST-PERSON POINT OF VIEW
> A literary style in which the *narrator* tells the story from his or her own *point of view* and refers to himself or herself as "I." The narrator may be an active participant in the story or just an observer.

HERO / HEROINE
> The principal *character* in a literary work or *narrative*.

IMAGERY
> Language that brings to mind sense-impressions, representing things that can be seen, smelled, heard, tasted, or touched.

MOTIF
> A recurring idea, structure, contrast, or device that develops or informs the major *themes* of a work of literature.

NARRATIVE
> A story.

LITERARY ANALYSIS

NARRATOR

The person (sometimes a *character*) who tells a story; the *voice* assumed by the writer. The narrator and the author of the work of literature are not the same person.

PLOT

The arrangement of the events in a story, including the sequence in which they are told, the relative emphasis they are given, and the causal connections between events.

POINT OF VIEW

The *perspective* that a *narrative* takes toward the events it describes.

PROTAGONIST

The main *character* around whom the story revolves.

SETTING

The location of a *narrative* in time and space. Setting creates mood or atmosphere.

SUBPLOT

A secondary *plot* that is of less importance to the overall story but may serve as a point of contrast or comparison to the main plot.

SYMBOL

An object, *character,* figure, or color that is used to represent an abstract idea or concept. Unlike an *emblem,* a symbol may have different meanings in different contexts.

SYNTAX

The way the words in a piece of writing are put together to form lines, phrases, or clauses; the basic structure of a piece of writing.

THEME

A fundamental and universal idea explored in a literary work.

TONE

The author's attitude toward the subject or *characters* of a story or poem or toward the reader.

VOICE

An author's individual way of using language to reflect his or her own personality and attitudes. An author communicates voice through *tone, diction,* and *syntax.*

LITERARY ANALYSIS

A NOTE ON PLAGIARISM

Plagiarism—presenting someone else's work as your own—rears its ugly head in many forms. Many students know that copying text without citing it is unacceptable. But some don't realize that even if you're not quoting directly, but instead are paraphrasing or summarizing, *it is plagiarism* unless you cite the source.

Here are the most common forms of plagiarism:

- Using an author's phrases, sentences, or paragraphs without citing the source
- Paraphrasing an author's ideas without citing the source
- Passing off another student's work as your own

How do you steer clear of plagiarism? You should *always* acknowledge all words and ideas that aren't your own by using quotation marks around verbatim text or citations like footnotes and endnotes to note another writer's ideas. For more information on how to give credit when credit is due, ask your teacher for guidance or visit www.sparknotes.com.

Review & Resources

Quiz

1. What does Simon Peter do for a living before he becomes an apostle?

   A. He is a carpenter.
   B. He is a fisherman.
   C. He is an itinerant preacher.
   D. He is a baker.

2. In the Gospel of Mark, how does the Virgin Mary learn of her pregnancy?

   A. There is no virgin birth in the Gospel of Mark.
   B. From the angel Gabriel
   C. Joseph learns of the news in a dream.
   D. Mary has a vision.

3. Who is Stephen in Acts of the Apostles?

   A. Paul's intern
   B. The first Christian martyr
   C. The founder of the church at Corinth
   D. One of the apostles

4. The author of Acts of the Apostles also wrote which of the four Gospels?

   A. Matthew
   B. Mark
   C. Sebastian
   D. Luke

5. According to the Gospel of Matthew, who visits Jesus at his birth and where does this meeting take place?

    A. The three wise men, in a stable
    B. Five shepherds, in a stable
    C. The three wise men, in a house
    D. Five shepherds, at a midwifery center in Palestine

6. By what name is Paul of Tarsus known before he begins his missionary activity?

    A. Simon
    B. Levi
    C. Saul
    D. Stephen

7. According to Paul's formulation in 1 Corinthians, which is the greatest of the imperishable qualities?

    A. Charity
    B. Chastity
    C. Hope
    D. Love

8. Who is the high priest of Jerusalem who put Jesus on trial?

    A. Caiaphas
    B. Pilate
    C. Herod
    D. Caesar

9. In the Gospel According to John, which of the apostles doubts Jesus's resurrection until he sees Jesus with his own eyes?

    A. Paul
    B. Thomas
    C. Judas
    D. Peter

10. In the Book of Revelation, who does the beast represent?

   A. Adulterous women
   B. The Roman Empire
   C. Nonbelievers
   D. Jesus when he returns

11. According to the Gospel of Matthew, where does Jesus's first public sermon take place?

   A. On the plain
   B. In Jerusalem
   C. In the temple
   D. On the mount

12. In the Gospel of John, for whom does Mary Magdalene mistake Jesus in his first resurrection appearance?

   A. Peter
   B. A gardener
   C. A ghost
   D. Her father

13. In Paul's letters to the Corinthians, what teaching is he trying to convey?

   A. Unity amidst diversity
   B. Sexual restraint
   C. Love as the most important virtue
   D. All of the above

14. How does Judas signal Jesus's identity to the Roman officials?

   A. He points to him.
   B. He kisses him.
   C. He hands them a drawing of him.
   D. He publicly pronounces Jesus's name.

15. Who discovers the empty tomb of Jesus?

   A.   Peter
   B.   Paul and Stephen
   C.   Judas
   D.   Mary Magdalene and Mary, mother of James and
        Joseph

16. Who murders John the Baptist?

   A.   Herod the Great
   B.   Ciaphas
   C.   Pilate
   D.   An angry mob

17. When Christians observe Palm Sunday, what biblical
    narrative are they celebrating?

   A.   Jesus's feeding of the 5,000
   B.   The Last Supper
   C.   Jesus's entry into Jerusalem before his death
   D.   The Sermon on the Mount

18. According to the Gospels, what is the unique literary genre
    Jesus employs to preach his message?

   A.   The parable
   B.   Mystery sayings
   C.   Comic-tragic drama
   D.   Proverbial sayings

19. Which Gospel is most concerned with the mystery and
    identity of the person of Jesus?

   A.   Matthew
   B.   John
   C.   Mark
   D.   James

20. Who baptizes Jesus?

    A. Mary
    B. Joseph
    C. John the Baptist
    D. Herod

21. Who takes Jesus's body off the cross?

    A. Joseph of Arimathea
    B. Peter
    C. Mary
    D. Martha

22. Who is the first apostle to deny Jesus?

    A. Judas
    B. Peter
    C. Mary
    D. Lazarus

23. Which part of the New Testament is written by Jesus?

    A. The Gospels
    B. Revelation
    C. Nothing in the New Testament is written by Jesus.
    D. Acts

24. When was the New Testament written?

    A. While Jesus was preaching and traveling
    B. Between 70 and 120 A.D.
    C. 300 A.D.
    D. 35 A.D.

REVIEW & RESOURCES

25. In what city was Jesus born?

    A. Nazareth
    B. Canaan
    C. Bethlehem
    D. Newark

ANSWER KEY

1: B; 2: A; 3: B; 4: D; 5: C; 6: C; 7: D; 8: A; 9: B; 10: B; 11: D; 12: B;
13: D; 14: B; 15: D; 16: A; 17: C; 18: A; 19: A; 20: B; 21: A; 22: A;
23: C; 24: B; 25: C

Suggestions for Further Reading

DULING, DENNIS C., and NORMAN PERRIN. *The New Testament: Proclamation and Parenesis, Myth and History*. New York: Harcourt College Publishers, 1994.

FELDER, CAIN HOPE. *Stony the Road We Trod: African American Biblical Interpretation*. Minneapolis: Fortress Press, 1991.

FREEDMAN, DAVID NOEL, ed. *The Anchor Bible Dictionary*. New York: Doubleday, 1998.

FIORENZA, ELISABETH SCHÜSSLER. *In Memory of Her: A Feminist Theological Reconstruction of Christian Origins*. New York: Crossroad Publishing Company, 10th Anniversary Edition, 1994.

HARRISVILLE, ROY A., and WALTER SUNDBERG. *Baruch Spinoza to Brevard Childs*. Grand Rapids, MI: Eerdmans Publishing, 2nd edition 2002.

MCDONALD, LEE M. *The Formation of the Christian Biblical Canon*. Peabody, MA: Hendrickson Publishers, 1995.

THEISSEN, GERD. *The Social Setting of Pauline Christianity: Essays on Corinth*. Edited and translated by John H. Schütz. Philadelphia: Fortress Press, 1982.

REVIEW & RESOURCES

SparkNotes Literature Guides

Visit sparknotes.com for many more!